GETTING IT RIGHT

Acknowledgments,
Contributors and Reviewers

*This reference manual could not have been completed
without the kindness and dedication to the field of family history
of those whose names are listed here:*

Gary Boyd Roberts, NEHGS
David Allen Lambert, Reference Library Manager,
Technology and Microtext Library, NEHGS
Elizabeth Shown Mills, CG, CGL, FASG, FNGS
Karen Clifford, GRA, Inc.
Dave Berdan, Legacy Family Tree Software
Ken McGinnis, Legacy Family Tree Software
Steve Cannon, PAF, TempleReady, Ancestral File
Ruth Inman, Medieval TempleReady Clearing
Glade Nelson, Family History Library,
British and International Reference and Catalogue
Debbie Latimer, Family History Library, Medieval Families Unit
Lynda Nixon, British Studies Specialist
Sandra Oman, Medieval Welsh Specialist
Egil Simonsen, Scandinavian Specialist
Heidi Sugden, French Specialist
Melanie Glazener, Irish Studies Specialist
Eva Gremert, Irish Clans Specialist
Laura Young
Kenneth Harmon, Temple Recorder Seattle Temple
Linda Osborne, Family File Seattle Temple
Donna Newell, Family File Seattle Temple
Ardyth Oien, Family File Seattle Temple
Kevin Richardson, Temple Recorder, Las Vegas Temple
Maureen Bryson, Family File Las Vegas Temple
Betty Topham, Family File Las Vegas Temple

Dedication

To Dean, Michael and Rachel

Getting It Right

THE DEFINITIVE GUIDE TO RECORDING FAMILY HISTORY ACCURATELY

MARY H. SLAWSON

Library of Congress Cataloging-in-Publication Data

Slawson, Mary H.
    Getting it right : the definitive guide to recording family history accurately / Mary H. Slawson
       p.   cm.
    Includes index.
    ISBN 1-57008-887-X (pbk.)
    1. Genealogy. 2. United States—Genealogy—Handbooks, manuals, etc. I. Title.
CS14 .S59 2002
929' .1'072073—dc21   2002011076

Printed in the United States of America   54459-7013
Malloy Lithographing Incorporated, Ann Arbor, MI

10   9   8   7   6   5   4   3   2

Contents

Introduction

If you are one of the millions of people who research, record, organize, or share family history, this book is for you. You are part of a vast community that spans continents and epochs, linking yourself through tangible records to your ancestors and eventually to your descendents. Unlike any other book on genealogy, *Getting it Right* is the definitive sourcebook of the rules and language you need in order for your research to fit smoothly and efficiently into the jigsaw puzzle of family histories that have been and are being assembled by others like you around the world. Use it as a style guide for all your data entry, and as a reference manual for your family research. You will save untold hours and increase the accuracy of your family records.

The genealogical information you compile from your ancestors' records may be recorded in a variety of genealogical software designed for that purpose, or on paper forms. The guidelines, terminology, and methods for working with your records described in this book are the same, regardless of the tools you use, except where otherwise noted.[1]

By investing the time to learn and consistently apply the information in this book, your family history will be optimized for use in both the most commonly used genealogy software and on paper, saving you and others countless hours of work and rework. *Getting it Right* will help you:

- Decrease the time needed to search through family history databases.
- Reduce errors and rework when erroneous submissions get rejected by online family history repositories such as Ancestry.com™, GENDEX™, Family File™, Ancestral File™, and TempleReady™.
- Increase the speed of merging family history databases.
- Standardize information used to identify your ancestors and record significant events in their lives.
- Make the sharing of information with family members and other researchers easier.

---

[1] Screen shots used in this book to illustrate computerized forms are based on the Legacy® Family Tree™ software program; however equivalent places to enter data exist in all the other major software packages, including PAF™, Family Origins™, Family Tree Maker™, and Master Genealogist™. All trademarks in this book belong to their owners.

The Motivation for This Book

I started researching my own family history in 1973, and through the years I have experienced the marvelous satisfaction that comes only from identifying and compiling the records and history of the members of one's own family. Whether you are young, old, a beginner, a hobbyist, or a semi-professional or professional genealogical researcher, this easy-to-understand style guide defines and explains the generally accepted standards for adding, organizing, maintaining, and sharing family history records in a consistent manner. From it you will learn the language of genealogy that you need in order for you—and your records—to participate in the world of family research.

The need for this book became apparent when I first attempted to merge (combine) two databases of over 250,000 names each, along with thousands of smaller files that were donated by researching members of a 700+-member family history organization in which I participate over the Internet. The task took over two years; mostly because of inconsistencies in the way people had recorded their family information.

Through a collaborative process over the Internet, my virtual family history organization eventually developed the underpinnings of a consistent style for recording and using information. With that as a starting point, I investigated and referenced hundreds of authoritative sources and, with the help of many experts and authorities in the field, I refined, expanded, and compiled into this book the complete set of generally accepted style and standards for working with family history.

Today, the growing membership of that same organization annually merges new information collected throughout the year and stored in a variety of software programs, including PAF™, Legacy, Family Origins™, Family Tree Maker™, Master Genealogist™, and others. The amount of new information collected by these researchers each year is staggering. But now the merge takes place in a matter of only one week using the guidelines described in *Getting it Right*. From this experience an important lesson was learned, which is:

> *While software can greatly improve the efficiency of managing data and working with other family historians, most of those efficiencies depend entirely on information being recorded and used in a consistent manner.*

While you may never have occasion to merge large family databases—and even if you do most or all of your family research on paper—the Internet and certain software programs have greatly accelerated the pace of research, the size and potential connectedness of collections, and the need for a systematic approach to *your* family history.

Someday, the ability for your record to be found by another researcher, even a future member of your own family, may depend on the degree to which you have adhered to the standards contained in this book. In the meantime, I sincerely hope and believe that your ability to find, enter, organize, maintain, share, and enjoy your collected family history will be greatly enhanced by your understanding and consistent application of the information contained in *Getting it Right*.

 —Mary H. Slawson
 http://GettingItRight.org

Organization: The Four Forms
Used to Compile Your Family History

Getting it Right describes each form used to compile a family history and explains how to enter data into each of the four forms that comprise the foundation of all genealogical research. Whether you are working on paper or on a computer, the four basic forms are:

- Family Group Record (FGR, also known as Family Group Sheet or the Family View in your software).
- Pedigree Chart.
- Research Log.
- Correspondence Log.

As you will see, the FGR is the first and most fundamental of family history forms. It deals with the recording of identities and events. The wide variety of historical styles of names and titles, place names, events, and other conventions as they have evolved over time makes for many reasons to standardize. These standards make up—by far—the largest portion of this book. Fear not, however. You will find that the information you need is clearly organized in each section, as well as indexed at the end of the book.

The Pedigree Charts, Research Logs, and Correspondence Log sections are smaller but equally important:

Pedigree charts summarize information from the FGR into a format that is suitable for seeing and discovering relationships easily, for working in the library, and for displaying and sharing your family tree. If you use software, you can generate pedigree charts automatically from FGR information in your database; however there are often many styles to choose from and the proper organization, advantages, and disadvantages of each kind are presented in that section. Also included in that section is a description of the kinds of information you will find in pedigree charts. If you are creating pedigree charts manually on paper, everything you need to know to properly organize, format, and use this kind of form and the information on it is described in this section.

Your **research log** is a record of where you have looked for information and what you found there.

Finally, your **correspondence log** is for keeping track of whom you talked with or corresponded with in your search for information.

Your proper and consistent use of the two log forms is essential for managing your work and building a meaningful and useful collection over time.

In doing family research you will be locating sources; finding and gathering information; entering, updating, and linking information in FGRs (paper FGR forms or the Family View of your software); and keeping logs of your research and correspondence. You also will be continually documenting your sources on the basic forms, whether working on paper or in related locations in your software.

This book is designed so that you can read it through from cover to cover, study individual sections, or look up information as you need it before you begin or during your task of documenting your family history.

I. Family Group Record

Recording information on a family group record (FGR) will be a lifelong process of acquiring and recording information about your ancestors. This section will discuss how to enter data about your ancestors on a paper Family Group Record[2] or in the Family View of your software. A FGR or Family View contains information about:

- A husband.
- A wife.
- The parents of a husband.
- The parents of a wife.
- Children.
- Other wives and husbands.
- Children's spouses.
- Birth dates and place names.
- Christening dates and place names.
- Death dates and place names.
- Burial dates and place names.
- Specific events.
- Notes.
- Documentation.

The information in the FGR deals with identity (names, titles, and gender) and events (dates, geographic locations, and event tags that indicate the kind of event). Identity elements uniquely identify individuals and can be used collectively to identify and record information about your ancestors in a family history database or a FGR. All data should be entered so that it is as comprehensive and clear as possible. Elements used for identity include:

- Names.
- Gender.
- Birth, christening, or baptism information.
- Death and burial information.
- Marriage information.
- Children.
- Events in your ancestor's life.
- General, research, and medical notes.

---

[2] Also sometimes called a Family Group Sheet.

None of the information used to substantiate the identity of your ancestor should be abbreviated.

Family Group Sheet

Husband	Charles Homer Fuller	
Born	23 Sep 1857	Danbury, Fairfield, Connecticut, USA
Christened	23 Nov 1857	
Died	1927	Brighton Town, Monroe, New York, USA
Buried		
Father	Azariel Charles Fuller (1836-1922)	Mother	Margaret L. Hawley (1844-1864)
Married		Utica, Oneida, New York, USA

Wife	Mary Jane Dwyer	
Born	15 Feb 1864	Utica, Oneida, New York, USA
Christened		
Died	1949	Rochester, Monroe, New York, USA
Buried	1949	Holy Sepulcher Cemetery, Rochester, Monroe, New York, USA
Father	James Dwyer (1822-)	Mother	Mary (1822-)

Children

1	M	George Henry Fuller	
Born	10 Apr 1884	Rochester, Monroe, New York, USA	
Christened			
Died	3 Aug 1957	Rochester, Monroe, New York, USA	
Buried	6 Aug 1957	Holy Sepulcher Cemetery, Rochester, Monroe, New York, USA	
Spouse	Sarah Fremouw (1882-1961)	4 Jul 1906 - Rochester, Monroe, New York, USA	

2	M	Raymond Fuller	
Born	15 Oct 1904	Rochester, Monroe, New York, USA	
Christened			
Died	12 Jun 1966	Rochester, Monroe, New York, USA	
Buried			
Spouse	Elizabeth Florence Bevan (1901- Abt 1985)	28 Apr 1928 - Rochester, Monroe, New York, USA	

3	M	Edward Joseph Fuller	
Born	14 Jul 1895	Utica, Oneida, New York, USA	
Christened			
Died	25 Oct 1947	Rochester, Monroe, New York, USA	
Buried			
Spouse	Mary Ana Zeitvogel (1901-)	26 Apr 1920 - Rochester, Monroe, New York, USA	

4	F	Elizabeth or Bessie Fuller	
Born	31 Jan 1898	Utica, Oneida, New York, USA	
Christened		Sacrament Church, Rochester, Monroe County, New York, USA	
Died	Sep 1978	Rochester, Monroe, New York, USA	
Buried	Sep 1978	Holy Sepulcher Cemetery, Rochester, Monroe, New York, USA	
Spouse	Thomas Clarence Mooney (Abt 1922-)	15 Jun 1950 - Utica, Oneida, New York, USA	

5	M	Frank J. Fuller	
Born	8 Jan 1888	Utica, Oneida, New York, USA	
Christened			
Died		Batavia, Genesee County, New York, USA	
Buried			
Spouse	Amanda Huff (Abt 1891-)	, , Pennsylvania, USA	

(continued on next page)

Figure 1. A Typical Family Group Record.

A. Names

An individual's name comprises as many as six elements. These elements are:

- Given names.
- Surnames.
- Nicknames.
- AKA (also known as) names, including:
  - Alternate spellings.
  - Pseudonyms.
  - Aliases.
- Title prefixes and suffixes.

Not all individuals have all these elements. The goal is to enter all that you can clearly identify and document regarding your ancestor.

Given Names

The given name is the individual's legal first name and middle name as they appear on a birth certificate, baptismal record, or other legal document filed with a public or religious institution.

The Use of *Formerly* and *Or*

It was once common practice when using family history software to use the words "formerly" and "or" between different spellings of a given name, different given names used by your ancestor, a legal name and a nickname, or other AKA names. This is no longer applicable when entering names in family history software. Instead, all alternate given and surnames are entered into the program's AKA field (sometimes called the alternate name field).

Exception: If using a paper FGR form, the words "formerly" and "or" are still used between alternate names.

Alternate Spellings

All alternate spellings of the given name should be entered in the AKA field of your software. The software is designed to accommodate a list of one or multiple entries. Be sure to include with each entry in the AKA field the surname along with the alternate spelling of the given name. This will make your database searches more efficient, assist you when merging family lines together, and help you avoid duplications. If you bury alternate spellings of a name in the notes field of your software you will not be able to take advantage of new indexing features that exist in some software programs today and are coming in others in the near future, allowing you search for all forms of your ancestor's name, and match and merge on these variations as well.

Example

For an ancestor whose given name is legally recorded as Wilhelm but was later recorded as William (having the given name anglicized), do the following:

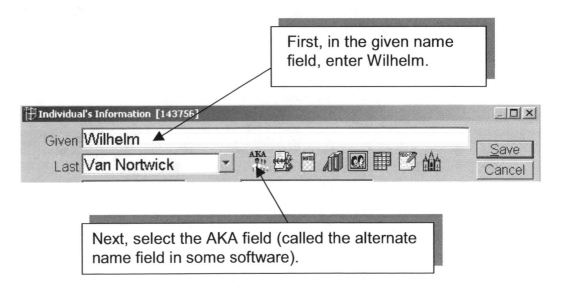

First, in the given name field, enter Wilhelm.

Next, select the AKA field (called the alternate name field in some software).

Then, enter William in the AKA given name field.

Add/Edit Alternate Name

Given Name: William

Last Name: Van Nortwick

Title Prefix: Title Suffix:

Save   Cancel

Finally, be sure to enter the surname.

🛈 Do not enter "Wilhelm or William" in the given name field; only "Wilhelm".

Individual's Information [143756]

Given: Wilhelm or William

Last: Van Nortwick

Save

Cancel

What Language to Use

The given name should be recorded in the language your ancestor used to record his or her own family name, or, if unknown, the language most likely used in the home or country of origin found in original documents[3]. It can become confusing when various sources provide different spellings, or translate names from other languages into English. Be careful; many family history sources record names in English that were originally recorded on documents in your ancestor's language. Do not use English unless your ancestor used it to record his or her name on original documents. Where an anglicized name (i.e., the English version of the name) is also found on source records, it should be entered into the AKA field.

---

[3] In order to enter family names or other information in various native languages into your software, your software must support the alphabet, or characters, used by a given language. Refer to appendix D, Other Languages in Your Software, for a general overview of features or settings you may need. Refer to your family history and operating system software documentation or online help as needed for details on installing software or features, or changing language settings that may be needed to support other languages.

If the name is not found in the language most likely used by your ancestor for signing documents or used in your ancestor's home or country of origin, and the name is only recorded in Latin, use the Latin given name in the given name field. If there is also an anglicized version of the name, enter it in the appropriate AKA field.

Example of what language to use

> Your ancestor came from Holland in 1620 and spoke and wrote his name in Dutch. Use the Dutch name Jan for the given name, not the English name John.
>
> If the anglicized name, John, is also found in documents, enter it along with the surname in the AKA field and document the source of your ancestor's anglicized name.

Recording Given Names

When entering the given name of your ancestor into your software or onto a paper FGR form, enter the first given name followed by any middle name or middle initial in the Given Name field. All given names should be spelled out in their entirety when known. Initials may be used when the full given name is not known.

Examples

> **Margaret Ann**
> **William James**
> **Benjamin A.**
> **B. J.**
> **W. Patrick**

Whenever possible, do not abbreviate given names.

> **Use William; do not use Wm.**
> **Use Jill St. Rose, rather than Jill Saint**
> **Rose, if that is how your ancestor**
> **spelled her name.**

When Surname Appears Before the Given Name

Some countries place the surname first and then the given names in their legal documents. All given names should be entered into the Given Name field of your family history software or the paper FGR form. For family history purposes, the given name is always entered into the Given Name field regardless of where it appears in a legal document. This includes both the first given name, like John or Rebecca, and any middle name or middle initial.

Capitalization and Punctuation

The first letter of all given names and initials should be capitalized. Unless your ancestor's birth or baptismal record does not use periods after initials, care should be taken to use a period after each initial used.

Example

> Use James R. (not James R)
> Use J. W. (not JW, JW., or J.W.)

Occasionally, an individual is legally given only initials for a given name. In this instance, enter the initials in the Given Name field and clarify your entry in the Notes field for the given name.

Example

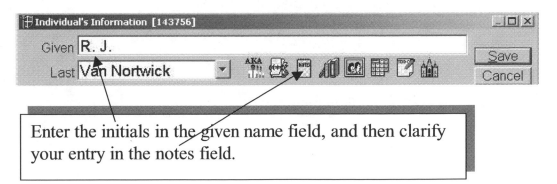

Enter the initials in the given name field, and then clarify your entry in the notes field.

When entering data in the Given Name field, do not include aliases, alternate spellings, occupations, descriptions, or titles.

Do not include any portion of a surname in the Given Name field. Refer to Surnames on page 41.

Patronymic names may only be entered in the Given Name field if the individual has a legal surname. All other patronymic names are entered in the surname field. Refer to Patronymic Surnames on page 44.

The Use of Special Symbols in Given Name Field

Never *italicize* in the Given Name field or use single quotation marks ' ', braces { } brackets [ ], question marks ?, or other symbols that are not part of the individual's legal name. The = symbol is not used to replace a dit; refer to usage of French Dits in Surnames on page 47.

Points of clarification usually intended by the use of special characters or symbols should be entered into either the general Notes field or the research Notes field of your family history software, or the Sources of Information (SI) field on a paper FGR form.

Parentheses ( ) are used in the Given Name field only to clarify the birth order of multiple children in the same family with the exact same name. Refer to Children With the Same Given Name on page 34.

Hyphens and apostrophes may be used if they are a part of the legal given name. Hyphens are also used if your ancestor took a new name when he or she became a nun or a monk and subsequently became known by a hyphenated given name consisting of the original name and the new name. The original name is entered in the Given Name field, and newer, hyphenated names are always entered in the AKA field with the earliest chronological name first (e.g., Philippi-Mathilde de Toulouse, Guy Geoffroy-Guillaume VI comte de Poitou). Hyphens are not used between alternate spellings of a name. These should be entered into your AKA field.

Quotation marks are used only in connection with certain types of nicknames. Refer to Nicknames in the next section.

Nicknames

There are three kinds of nicknames to consider when recording your ancestor's information:

- Nicknames used as replacements for a given name, including given names that have been shortened and affectionate pet names.
- Nicknames that are descriptive (usually based on an obvious characteristic of your ancestor).
- Names commonly used as nicknames that, in the case of your ancestor, were used as the legal given name.

Each of the three types of nicknames is recorded differently.

ⓘ When recording a nickname in the Given Name field, never *italicize* or use single quotation marks ' ', braces { }, brackets [ ], question marks ?, or other symbols that are not part of the individual's legal name. Nicknames are sometimes entered with double quotation marks " " as explained below (refer to Exception for Irish Names in the next section, and Nicknames as Descriptions on page 26).

Nicknames as Replacements

The most common type of nickname is when your ancestor's legal given name has been abbreviated or replaced with a shorter given name or affectionate pet name. Whenever an individual is known by a replacement nickname, indicate the legal given name in the Given Name field, and then enter the nickname in the AKA field. When using a paper FGR form, this kind of nickname is entered into the Notes field.

ⓘ Do not use quotation marks " " around nicknames used as abbreviations or replacements for a given name (i.e., do not enter "Billie" with quotation marks when Billie is a replacement nickname for William).

Exception: Irish names frequently are accompanied by recognized legal nicknames that are used very commonly in place of the given name, on legal documents such as school transcripts and marriage licenses. Irish nicknames should not be entered in the AKA field. Instead, enter the nickname—in quotation marks—following the legal given name in the Given Name field. This is true regardless of whether the Irish nickname is an abbreviation, replacement, or descriptive type of nickname. See Nicknames as Descriptions, below, for an example of the proper use of quotation marks. If you do not know the legal given name for your Irish ancestor, but you know the nickname, enter the nickname by itself, in quotation marks, in the Given Name field.

Example of Irish Nickname Exception

If you do not know the legal given name for your non-Irish ancestor, but you do know the abbreviation or replacement nickname, leave the Given Name field blank and enter the gender and surname in the appropriate fields; then enter the abbreviation or replacement nickname in the AKA field without using quotation marks around the name. Refer also to Unknown Given Names on page 28.

Examples of entering nicknames as replacements for legal given names

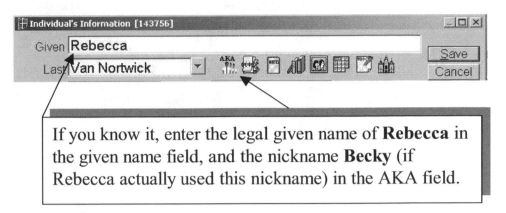

If you know it, enter the legal given name of **Rebecca** in the given name field, and the nickname **Becky** (if Rebecca actually used this nickname) in the AKA field.

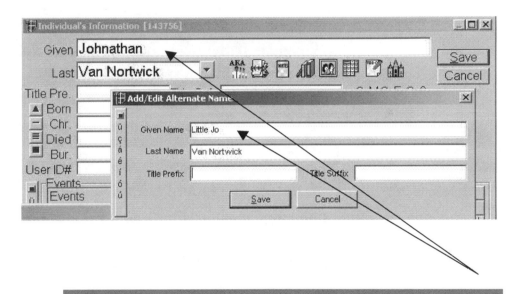

When you find additional nicknames, add them to your existing list of AKAs. For example, enter Jonathan in the given name field and Little Jo in the AKA field. Remember to enter the surname in the surname field of each AKA entry.

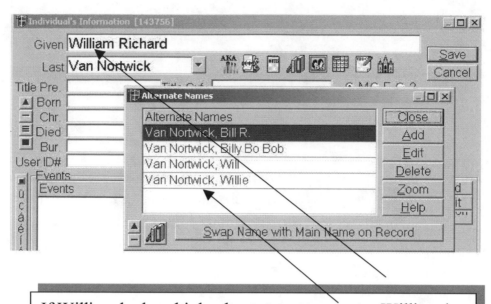

> If William had multiple alternate names, enter William in the given name field; then add all the nicknames William used (e.g., Bill R., Billy Bo Bob, Will, and Willie) as separate entries in the AKA field. Use the surname with each AKA entry.

Nicknames as Descriptions

Royal, Irish, Egyptian, Mesopotamian, and Viking lines are examples of lines that commonly use nicknames as adjectives or descriptions. This kind of nickname usually describes a quality of character, a physical attribute, or a military act by which your ancestor has become well known (for better or worse!). A name can include a roman numeral to designate the sequence of usage of a given name by a series of rulers or religious leaders. (Refer to appendix A, Roman Numerals, on page 221.) In these cases the given name is entered first, followed by the Roman numeral, then by the nickname, all in the Given Name field.

Nicknames used as descriptions are *always* set apart by double quotation marks " ". No other special symbols are used in the Given Name field. Refer to The Use of Special Symbols in the Given Name Field on page 21 and the use of French Dits on page 47.

Examples of entering nicknames that are descriptions

Individual's Information [143756]

Given | Richard "the kingmaker"
Last | Neville
Title Pre. | Title Suf. earl of Warwick   M C E C ?
Save
Cancel

Individual's Information [143756]

Given | John III "the red"
Last | Comyn
Title Pre. | Title Suf. lord of Badenoch   M C E C ?
Save
Cancel

Nicknames as Legal Given Names

When a name that is commonly used as a nickname is given to a child as their legal first or middle name on a birth certificate, baptismal record, or other legal document filed with a public or religious institution, enter it in the Given Name field. Then make a notation in the given name Notes field to make it clear that you intended this to be entered as the given name. Refer also to Pseudonyms and Alternate Spellings of Given Names on page 39.

Example of nickname used as legal given name

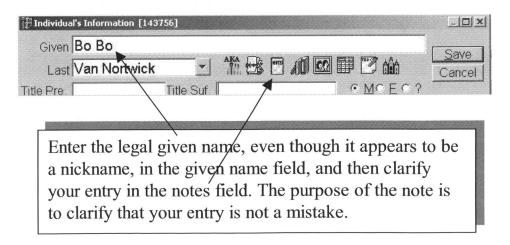

Enter the legal given name, even though it appears to be a nickname, in the given name field, and then clarify your entry in the notes field. The purpose of the note is to clarify that your entry is not a mistake.

27

Unknown Given Names

Many genealogical records do not contain the full names of our ancestors. Some individuals are recorded without their first or middle name, or both. The following will assist you in recording these cases of missing information.

Unknown Given Name and Gender

When a child was stillborn or died within a few days of birth, or that child's records or tombstone does not include a given name, it may become necessary to enter the child as an unnamed child into your records. If the child was not given a given name and you know the gender, enter a male child as such. Leave the given name blank and enter the surname only. To enter an unnamed female child, enter "Miss" in the Given Name field and the maiden name in the surname field. When you cannot identify the gender of the child, leave the Given Name field blank, then enter the surname, and then select unknown for the gender. If using a paper FGR form, enter "U" for the gender, if unknown. Refer also to Gender on page 110.

Details regarding miscarriages are not entered in the children's name fields; instead, this information is entered in the Notes field under medical records for the mother. Refer to Medical event tag on page 167.

Example of entering an individual when both the given name and gender are unknown.

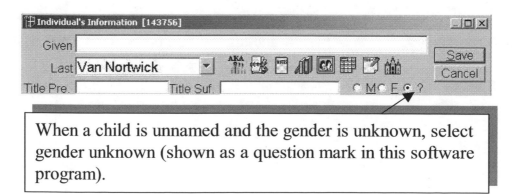

When a child is unnamed and the gender is unknown, select gender unknown (shown as a question mark in this software program).

Missing Given Names for Males

If you have neither the first name, nor a middle name, of your male ancestor, but you have other data such as a birth date, death date, or place, leave the Given Name field blank and enter the gender and surname and other relevant data in their respective fields.

At one time it was common practice to enter "Mr." (or the equivalent title in another language) if the given name was unknown. Mr. is no longer used when recording family history data. If you do not have any other information than the surname for a male, do not make a record for that individual unless either of the following cases occur (in either case, do not enter "Mr." or the equivalent):

1. The surname changed from parent to child.

2. The child was unnamed.

Example of entering a male when the given name is unknown

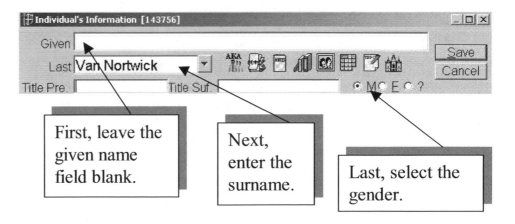

First, leave the given name field blank.

Next, enter the surname.

Last, select the gender.

29

(i) Do not enter words, peerage numbers, or phrases such as the following in the Given Name field for a male when the given name is unknown; it is understood that by leaving the field blank, you do not know the given name.

Do not enter words like these in the Given Name field:

- Baby
- Boy
- Child
- Gentilissimo Signore
- Infant
- Jr. or Junior
- Mr.
- Monsieur
- N.N.
- No Given Name
- The numbers 1st, 2nd, 3rd, etc. (These are reserved for use in the title field to indicate the order of peerage.)
- Captain, Governor, Doctor, or any other occupational titles
- Sr. or Senior
- Señor
- Stillborn
- Unknown
- Unnamed

Using *Daughter Of* or *Son Of*

"Daughter of" and "Son of" are not used to replace a missing given name unless that is how your ancestor is specifically described in original source materials. "Daughter of" or "Son of" is entered into the Given Name field followed by the parent's given name (or title, if no given name is provided in the source materials). Individuals recorded using "Daughter of" or "Son of" should not be submitted to TempleReady until the actual given name has been determined. For information on recording a patronymic name, refer to Patronymic Surnames on page 44.

Example of using **daughter of** *or* **son of**

Your original source indicates that Mor Nail married the daughter of the pharaoh of Egypt and you want to enter her information. You would enter "Daughter of pharaoh of Egypt" in the Given Name field in lieu of any other information.

Individual's Information [143756]	_ □ ×
Given Daughter of pharoah of Egypt	Save
Last [ ] ▼ 🔲🔲🔲🔲🔲🔲🔲🔲	Cancel

Using Miss

When the given names for your female ancestor are missing or unknown, "Miss" may be entered into the Given Name field, but only if followed by the maiden name in the surname field. Miss is always used with the maiden name, whether entering your ancestor as a wife or as a child.

If both the maiden name and the given name for your female ancestor are unknown, do not create a record for this individual. Other information you have regarding this individual is entered into the Notes field of the spouse or parent until you have a documented given name or surname.

Note: In the case of an unmarried female with a missing given name who comes from a non-English household, you should use the appropriate term in place of Miss in the Given Name field (e.g., Frauline, Mademoiselle, or Señorita, instead of Miss), followed by the maiden name.

ⓘ Do not enter words such as the following in the Given Name field for a female when the given name is unknown; it is understood that by entering "Miss", you do not know the given name.

Do not enter words like these in the Given Name field:

- Baby
- Child
- Girl
- Infant

- Ms.
- N.N.
- No Given Name

- Occupational titles
- Stillborn Children
- Unknown
- Unnamed

Using Mrs.

Mrs. is not entered in the place of a missing given name or missing given name and missing maiden name unless your ancestor is identified only as a widow in source materials. When your ancestor is recorded only as a widow, enter the abbreviation "Mrs." followed by the given name of the spouse, and then enter the spouse's surname where you would normally have entered your ancestor's maiden name.

Example of using Mrs.

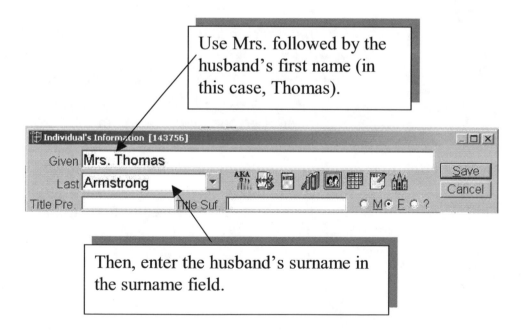

Use Mrs. followed by the husband's first name (in this case, Thomas).

Then, enter the husband's surname in the surname field.

Note: In the case of widows with missing given names and missing maiden names, who come from non-English households, you should use the appropriate term in place of Mrs. in the Given Name field (e.g., Frau, Fru, Madame, Distinta Signora, or Señora, instead of Mrs.).

If any portion of the given name is known and you do not know the maiden name, enter the given name in the Given Name field and leave the surname field blank. Do not use Miss or Mrs. or similar terms when any portion of the given name is known. If only the maiden name is known, refer to the use of Miss, above.

Missing Middle Name

Your ancestor may have come from a country or culture that traditionally gives children both a first name and a middle name. There are occasions when you want to record that you are missing the middle name for your ancestor or that the parents did not give their child a middle name.

If you know that the individual did not receive a middle name at birth and has no legal middle name, then make an entry in your Notes field explaining that the child has no middle name and indicate your source of information.

If you are missing a middle name for your ancestor, enter the first given name you do have, then leave the rest of the Given Name field blank. Next, indicate that you are missing the given middle name in the Notes field. If using a paper FGR form to record information regarding the status of a middle name, enter the information in the SI field or on the back of the FGR form.

Do not enter "no middle name given" or "missing middle name" in the Given Name field.

Unusual Given Name

Occasionally, a male is given a name that is usually considered a female name, such as Beverly, or, a female is given a name that is usually considered a male name, such as Lee. Or the name may be unusual in some other way. Enter the name into the Given Name field as usual. Then make a notation in the Notes field to clarify the entry and to document the unusual nature of the name. If using a paper FGR form, you should also underline the name. The goal is to make it clear that you did not made a mistake when entering the unusual name.

Children's Names

List all children, living or dead, in their order of birth (first-born child first, second-born child next, etc.). List the name of the child's spouse if you know it.

Note: If you are using a paper FGR form, you will also want to create a separate FGR form for each of the married children. When using software, the separate records for married children will be created automatically.

If there are more children than there are spaces provided for children on the paper FGR form, use a second sheet listing the same parents and continuing the numbering of the children.

Children With the Same Given Name

Occasionally, multiple children in a family are given the same given names. When this happens, record each child's given name, birth dates and death dates if you have them, then clarify the birth order by entering the child's place in the family in the Title Suffix field using "(1)" for the first child, "(2)" for the second child, "(3)" for the third child, and so on. This will prevent you from accidentally merging these children together as the same individual.

Example of children with the same given name in the same family

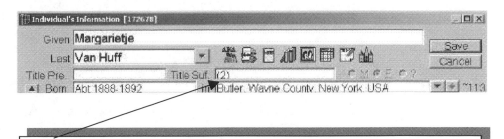

A (2) is entered to indicate that this Margarietje is the second child in the family to be given that name by her parents. This notation is entered in the title suffix field in parentheses.

ⓘ Do not use ordinal numbers (1st, 2nd, 3rd, First, Second, Third or I, II, III, etc.) to indicate birth order within a given family for children with the same name. These are reserved to clarify the order of monarchs and lords of feudal manors for specific countries or to enter the birth order in a family line. Refer to Titles event tag on page 179.

Children Named After Consecutive Ancestors

Many family lines use the same given names one generation after another. To avoid accidentally merging the consecutive generations of individuals together in your database, the child's place in the family line should be indicated whenever the names are exactly the same from one generation to the next. For example, when a father and son have the exact same name, "Senior" is entered in the Title Suffix field for the father, and "Junior" is added in the Title Suffix field of the child's record. If a son has the same name as his father and grandfather, the first generation uses the Roman numeral "I", the second uses "II", the third uses "III", etc. This information is entered first in the Title Suffix field, followed by any other titles. Refer to appendix A, Roman Numerals, on page 221 for a list of Roman numerals.

Roman numerals can also be used in the Given Name field to specify the order of ruling monarchs or feudal lords. Refer to Titles event tag on page 179. Examples of both types of usage are given below.

Examples of use in title suffixes field

In this example you are recording Robert Armstrong, Senior, Robert Armstrong, Junior, and Robert Armstrong, the III, all born in consecutive generations. A separate record is made for each individual, distinguishing each generation by indicating his place in the consecutive family line.

Make it clear that this is Robert Armstrong, Senior, by entering Senior in the title suffix field.

Indicate that this is Robert Armstrong, Junior, by entering Junior in the title suffix field.

Indicate that this is Robert Armstrong, III, by entering III in the title suffix field.

ⓘ Do not use ordinal numbers (1ˢᵗ, 2ⁿᵈ, 3ʳᵈ, First, Second, Third, or (1), (2), (3)) in the Given Name field. These terms are used only in the Title Suffix field to clarify the order of monarchs, lords of feudal manors for specific countries, or the birth order for siblings with exactly the same name. Refer to Titles event tag on page 179.

Examples of Roman numerals used in Given Name field

In the following example, Roman numerals are used to record individuals with the same name in a royal or feudal line to indicate their place in the family line. This is done in the Given Name field, directly after the given name. Frequently, the same name may skip a generation as in the case given below where Theobald III De Blois is the grandfather, and Theobald IV is his grandson.

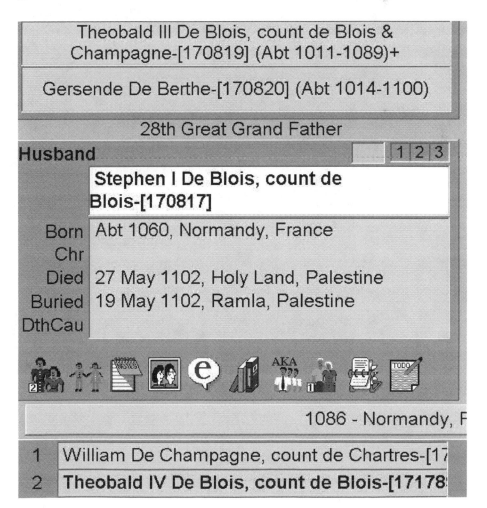

37

Children's Status Tags

The following status tags are used to describe a child's relationship to the recorded parents, to indicate a child was born dead, or a ward of guardians. These tags should not be abbreviated and should be entered in the child status field of your software, or after the surname on a paper FGR. "Possible" and "probable" are used to indicate the strength of evidence when recording a child as a member of a family unit when conclusive evidence is missing.

Adopted	Probable	Twin
Biological	Sealing	Unmarried
Foster	Stepdaughter	Ward
Illegitimate	Stepson	
Possible	Stillborn	

Example of use of Children's Status Tags

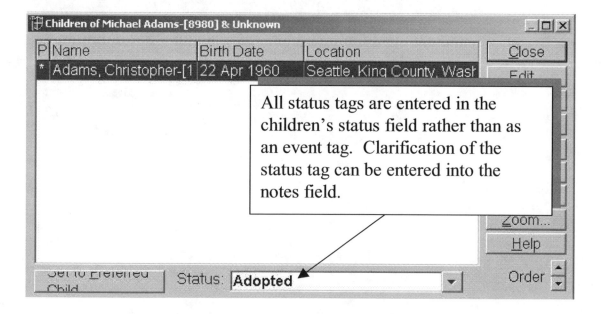

All status tags are entered in the children's status field rather than as an event tag. Clarification of the status tag can be entered into the notes field.

Pseudonyms and Alternate Spellings of Given Names

An individual may be known by one or more assumed names, including a pen name, a false name (pseudonym), or a stage name; or by alternate spellings of his or her given name. Alternate spellings are commonly a result of:

- Name changes when migrating from one country to another.
- Recording errors such as misspellings made by clerks and census takers.
- Illiteracy, or difficulties incurred by those spelling the name in the language used by your ancestor.

All assumed names and alternate spellings of a given name should be entered into the AKA or alternate name field of your software. The first name given at birth is entered into the given names field. All subsequent assumed names used are entered in the AKA fields. When entering names taken for first communion, becoming a nun or a priest, or other religious identification, enter the name given at birth in the Given Name field. Next, in the AKA fields, enter the new religious name taken. If your ancestor used hyphens between their legal and religious names you may do so in the AKA fields. In all cases you will want to document in your source notes where you acquired the alternate spelling. See also Nicknames on page 23.

When using a paper FGR form, the word "or" may be used between the alternate names in the Given Name field. If there are numerous alternate spellings of a given name and you run out of space, use the notes area or back of the form to record and make any necessary explanations. Record the source for each pseudonym or alternate spelling you record.

Note: When using the alternate name field in your software, you should always add the surname to the surname field associated with each alternate spelling of the given name. This will make your database searches more efficient and help you avoid unwanted duplications.

Example of entering pseudonyms or alternate spellings of a given name

Your ancestor's legal given name was Paulis Van Nortwick, which was found on a birth certificate. It was also how your ancestor usually signed his own name. Upon reading an old family bible plate, you discover that a family relative recorded your ancestor as Paul Noordwick. After completing additional research, you find a baptismal record at the Old Dutch church in Mamouth, New Jersey, and discover your ancestor was also known as Pullise Abramse Van Noordwickie. To record all these variations in the spelling of your ancestor's name, you would enter the information in the following manner:

First, enter Paulis in the given name field, and Van Nortwick in the surname field. Then, add each spelling variation in the AKA field.

Note that Pullise Abramse Van Noordwickie will also be known as just Pullise Abramse because the Dutch—in their record keeping—did not always use the surname or name of the feudal manor from which the family came. By entering each variation, the next time you want to enter data for this ancestor you will be able to search your database for all the variations.

Surname, Family Name, Last Name

The surname name is the individual's legal last name as it appears on a birth certificate, baptismal record, or other legal document filed with a public or religious institution. It is sometimes referred to as the family name. A surname is an inherited name used by all male members of a familial line and their unmarried children. When female children marry, their family name becomes known as their maiden name. On occasion, a surname may be derived from the mother's line in matriarchal societies or in the case of illegitimate children. Special care needs to be taken to document these uses.

The surname should be recorded in the language your ancestor used to record his or her own family name, or, if unknown, the language most likely used in the home or country or origin.[4] It can become confusing when various sources provide different spellings, or translate names from other languages into English names. Be careful: many family history sources record names in English that should have been recorded in your ancestor's language. Do not use English unless your ancestor used it to record his or her name on original documents. Where an anglicized name (i.e., the English version of the name) is also found on source records, it should be entered into the alternate name field.

If the name is not found in the language most likely used by your ancestor when signing documents or used in your ancestor's home, and the name is recorded only in Latin, use the Latin surname in the surname field. If there is also an anglicized version (i.e., the English language version) of the name, enter it in the appropriate AKA field.

Your ancestor's surname should be spelled out in its entirety, not abbreviated, unless your ancestor used an abbreviation in his or her surname (e.g., "St. John" or "St. Leger").

---

[4] To be able to enter family names or other information in various native languages into your software, your software must support the alphabet or "characters" used by a given language. Refer to appendix D, Other Languages in Your Software, for a general overview of features or settings you may need. Refer to your family history and operating system software documentation or online help as needed for details on installing software or features, or changing language settings, that may be needed to support other languages.

Surnames are recorded in the surname field of the family view of your software. When using a paper FGR form, record the surname after the given names in the name field.

Surnames in Uppercase or Lowercase

Surnames are *only* recorded using a mixture of uppercase and lowercase letters, as they appear in source documents. Your ancestors' surnames should be recorded using a mixture of capitalization and lowercase letters exactly as they recorded their own names. It was formerly common practice to record surnames in all uppercase on paper FGR forms used by the Church of Jesus Christ of Latter-day Saints; however, this practice is no longer applicable.

Note: It is still fashionable to use all uppercase surnames for book publication; however, modern family history software can automatically convert your properly recorded uppercase and lowercase surnames to all uppercase as desired when publishing.

Multiple Surnames

Some cultures, such as Hispanic, Native American and Tongan, for example, legally give their children multiple surnames at birth. If your ancestor was given multiple surnames, record all the surnames as one long entry in the surname field of your software, with each surname separated by a single space. When using a paper FGR form, enter the given names first, then all the legal surnames (e.g., "Manuel Diez Rodriguez Lopez").

Alternate Surnames

The surname that appears on your ancestor's birth or baptismal record is entered first into the surname field. All other surnames used are entered into the AKA field along with the given name for each surname. For additional information on the use of aliases, assumed names, and spelling variations of surnames, refer to Pseudonyms and Alternate Spellings of Given Name on page 39.

Maiden Names and Hyphenated Surnames

Record the maiden name of a female in the surname field.

If your female ancestor used a hyphenated surname that included her maiden name, list the maiden name by itself in the surname field. Next, enter the complete, hyphenated surname, including the maiden name, in the AKA field. When using a paper FGR form, enter the maiden name after all given names. On paper forms, if your female ancestor used a hyphenated surname that included her maiden name, list the maiden name in the surname field followed by the word "or", then record the full, hyphenated surname.

Examples of entering maiden and hyphenated surnames

Janette Johansen married Paul Van Nortwick and took on a hyphenated maiden name–married name as her legal name. Janette's maiden name of "Johansen" is entered in the surname field. Then, the hyphenated married name ("Johansen-Van Nortwick") is entered in the AKA field.

Different Surnames Within a Family

Members of the same family may have different surnames. This is most commonly found when an ancestor migrates from one country to another, resulting in spelling differences or wholesale changes in the surname.

It also frequently occurs when different sons inherit different estates and/or feudal manors upon the death of their father, and the sons' surname becomes a reference to the new estate or manor. Enter the surname legally used by each member of the family even though they may be different. Refer also to the Surname event tag on page 178.

When Surname Precedes Given Name

In some countries the surname is written first and the given names follow. For family history purposes, the surname is always recorded in the surname field regardless of where it appears in a legal document.

Patronymic Surnames

A patronymic surname is a name that has been derived from the given name of the father or other paternal ancestor. The father's given name becomes the child's surname, with the addition of a word meaning "daughter of" or "son of" appearing between the child's given name and the ancestor's name.

Example of patronymic surnames

The following is an example of three generations of a father, a son, and the son's daughter. The grandfather's name is Anharawd Ap Tangwydd. Anharawd is the given name. Ap Tangwydd is a patronymic surname. His son's name is Gawnan Ap Anharawd. Gawnan is the given name and Ap Anharawd is the patronymic surname derived from his father's given name. Gawnan's daughter is named Gudbjörg Gawnansdotter. Her patronymic surname is derived

44

from her father's given name and indicates the child is the daughter of—rather than the son of—Gawnan.

If your ancestor has a patronymic surname (e.g., Ap Tangwydd), it should be entered into the surname field of the family view or paper FGR form.

Exception: When, in addition to his or her patronymic name, your ancestor legally added a surname, the patronymic name should be entered into the Given Name field. For example, if your ancestor's given name was Gruffydd, and patronymic name was Ap Owain, and the legally added surname was De La Pole, your ancestor's full name became Gruffydd Ap Owain De La Pole. In the Given Name field, enter the given name (Gruffydd) followed by the patronymic name (Ap Owain). Then, in the surname field, enter the additional legal surname (De La Pole).

Table 1. Examples of Patronymic Surnames

Ap	ap Antonius	Ibn	Ibn 'Abdullah
Bat	bat Baraki'il	Mac	Mac Donald
Ben	ben Samathaiel	Mc	Mc Allister
Bint	bint Zelophehad	Se	Volkertse
Datter	Alfsdatter	Ze	Folkertze
Dotter	Bernadotter	Sen	Andriessen
Dottir	Algautsdottir	Son	Biornsson
Ferch	ferch Cadwaladr	Verch	verch Mathonwy
Fitz	Fitz Gerald		

45

Surnames Using Articles or Contractions

Arabic, Dutch, French, German, Portuguese, and Spanish surnames frequently use articles and contractions as a part of the surname. When articles or contractions are included in your ancestor's legal name, they should be retained, capitalized, and entered into the main surname field. If variations of the name with alternate spellings or contractions are used in your ancestor's line, those should be added in the AKA field.

Table 2. Examples of Articles and Contractions Used With Surnames

A'	Aus	La	Of
Ab	D'	Las	Ten
Abd	De	L'	Ter
Abdul	Des	Le	Van
Abdel	Di	Les	Van der
Abu	Du	Ler	Ver
Ad	El	Lo	Von
Al	Fer	O'	Zu
Av	Ibn		

As surnames that used these articles and contractions became anglicized over time, the articles may have been omitted or collapsed into the surname. To record surnames that include these elements, first enter the surname into the main surname field on the family view using the actual spelling that your ancestor used, including any spaces or punctuation.

Then, enter into the surname field of the AKA field any alternate spellings and punctuations for that surname that were used by your ancestor or other family members in the same line. Even if your ancestor did not use these variant spellings himself or herself, the addition of these alternate spellings from your family line into the AKA fields will help you when researching your lines, finding your ancestor in the Family File or other online family history databases, and merging your database with others. Clarify these entries in your

Notes field so you can keep track of AKA's your ancestor used and ones you are using for research purposes.

Example

> Individual's Information [143756]
>
> Given | Silas
> Last | Vanderveer
> Title Pre. | Title Suf. | M E ?
>
> Save
> Cancel

> **Silas Vanderveer** would be entered as **Vanderveer** in the main surname field of your family view and as Silas **Van Der Veer** and Silas **Vander Veer** in the AKA field.

French Dits

A French "dit," also known less frequently as a "soubriquet," is a name attached to a surname usually used to distinguish one family line from another who both live in the same locale. The dit could be derived from maiden names, locations, occupation, personality, physical features, or feats of skill and bravery. As the French migrated to England, Scotland, French Canada, and French-speaking communities in the United States, they brought the practice of using dits with them. All French dits are entered into the surname field.

Example of use of a French dit

In the case of Jarreti Fremouw dit Noir, Fremouw dit Noir would be entered into the surname field. Variant forms of the surname your ancestor used throughout his or her life would be entered into the AKA field.

 Do not use Fremouw=Noir in the surname field.

47

Missing Surnames

Born After 1600 A.D.

If your ancestor was born after 1600 and was not a slave, and you do not know his or her surname, leave the surname field blank. For missing female surnames, also refer to the use of Miss and Mrs. on pages 31 and 32.

If your ancestor was a slave and did not have a legal surname, you may enter one of the following. Options have been listed in the order of desirability (with the most desirable option first).

1. The surname of the owner on the first bill of sale.
2. The surname of the owner in whose will your ancestor was named.
3. When you cannot identify an owner but you can identify the plantation your ancestor lived on, the name of the plantation, which is entered in the surname field followed by the word "plantation".

Example of entering a slave born after 1600 without a surname

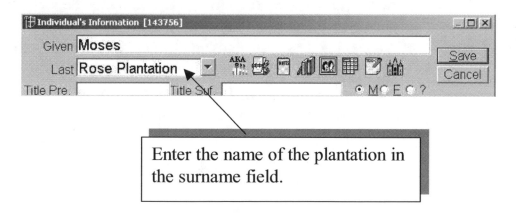

Enter the name of the plantation in the surname field.

Born Before 1600 A.D.

The practice of using a surname has evolved over time. Thus, in many instances, your ancestor many not have had a legal surname. If your ancestor was born prior to 1600 and you are missing a legal surname for that ancestor, you may enter one of the following. The options are listed in the order of desirability (with the most desirable option first). Information is also included for ancestors who were slaves in the section above. If items 1 through 5 below do not apply to your ancestor, leave the surname field blank.

1. Patronymic Names

If your ancestor is missing a legal surname but has a patronymic name, use the patronymic name as the missing surname. For a full description of the use of patronymic names refer to page 44.

2. Peerage Title

If your ancestor did not have a surname and had a peerage title, leave the surname field blank. The given name, the Roman numeral (if there is one), and nickname (if there is one) are entered into the Given Name field. The peerage title is entered into the Title Prefix and Title Suffix fields. Refer to Titles event tag on page 179.

3. Cities, Counties, Provinces, Regions, or Countries of Origin

Frequently, in records prior to 1500, individuals are recorded using their place of origin to help identify them. In these cases, the place of origin can be used in the surname field if the referenced location is a:

- Village, town, or city.
- County or province.
- Large geographic region.
- Country.

49

This entry is always preceded by the word "of" (or its equivalent in the native language) so that there is no confusion with an actual legal surname that also happens to be a location name (e.g. John England). In the example below, Albi is the place of origin and D' represents the word 'of' in the native language.

Example of a place of origin surname

4. Castles, Feudal Estates, and Manors

If your ancestor did not have a patronymic name or a peerage title, you can use the place of birth in the surname field if the birth was in a castle, feudal estate, or feudal manor.

Enter the word "of" (or its equivalent in the native language), followed by the name of the castle, estate, or manor.

Note: If also entering a place of birth or death, the word "Castle" can come before or after the actual name of the castle based on the local naming custom for the castle. "Estate" or "Manor" always follows the name of the feudal location.

50

Example of entering a castle, feudal estate, or manor in the surname field

5. Band or Tribal Names

Many cultures do not use a given name followed by a surname. For all cultures, the goal is to record your ancestor as he or she referred to himself or herself or as others called him or her.

For example, some Native American and African cultures may use naming conventions that include names of animals, geographic features, elements found in nature, or physical characteristics, such as Bright Hawk or He Who Runs Like Elk. Prior to European colonization, most indigenous populations used their own naming conventions that consisted of the following elements in the following order: A name, a place within a family structure, a place within a community or village, a name of a band of communities that affiliated with each other in trade or extended family relationships, the name of the tribe, and the name of the nation. The nations usually have little or nothing to do with geopolitical boundaries used today.

Not all cultures utilized every level in their naming conventions. The following is a general approach you can use as a guide for recording your ancestor who lived when non-European or nonpatronymic naming conventions were used, which follows the smallest family unit of self to the largest family organization of nation. The term "gen" is used by some Native American nations denoting lines of descent.

51

Naming conventions may change over time as a culture comes in contact with a more dominant culture. The following rules generally apply to entering band or tribal names:

Enter in the Given Name field:

Name called by, gen, clan, sub-band, and band

Enter in the surname field:

Tribe, and nation

Examples of entering band or tribal names

Enter in Given Name Field	Enter in Surname Field
Bright Hawk Payabya Oglala	Lakota Sioux
Hepan	Abdowapuskiyapi Dakota
Black Horse Itazipacola	Lakota Sioux

Scandinavian, Irish, and Scottish clan names are entered into the AKA fields in the suffix title field. Patronymic names are used for these lines until the first ancestor is recorded who uses the clan name as a legal surname.

Example of entering a clan name

In this example, Finnion is your oldest known ancestor and his son is Dwuane Mc Finnion. Dwuane is recorded as "Dwuane" in the Given Name field and "Mc Finnion" in the surname field. Dwuane's son Patrick Mc Dwuane is recorded as "Patrick" in the Given Name field and "Mc Dwuane" in the surname field. This patronymic naming continues down the family line until family members of the line begin to use a clan name.

When the family line becomes affiliated with a clan name, such as O'Brien or O'Kelly, enter the clan name as "Clan O'Brien" or "Clan O'Kelly" in the *AKA* title field. Do not enter a clan name in the surname field until your family line begins using a clan name (like O'Brien) as a surname.

Once the line uses the clan name as a surname, enter the given name and patronymic name if provided in the Given Name field, and then enter the surname (now O'Brien) in the surname field. Finally document the source materials used to determine the use of the clan name as a surname.

B. Titles and Offices

Most computer programs now have Title Prefix and Title Suffix fields.

Title prefixes are those that appear before the given name. The use of most title prefixes is optional. Each word in a title prefix is capitalized if used.

Examples of title prefixes and suffixes

Capitalize the start of each word in a title prefix. Most title prefixes are optional.

Title suffixes are those that appear after the surname. All title suffixes are always completely spelled out. No abbreviations are used. Capitalization depends on the type of title suffix used, as described below. The title suffix in the example below is "earl of Redhill."

The Order to Use When Entering Multiple Titles

The following order is used when entering title suffixes. **Note:** The designations "widow" and "twins" are recorded in the Notes field. They are not entered in the title fields.

- **(1), (2), (3)**—A child's place within a given family.

- **Senior, Junior, III, IV,** etc.—A child's place within the family line. Senior and Junior should be spelled out in the Title Suffix field.

- **Military Officer Titles, including Knighthood**

- **Peerage Titles**—The highest peerage title is used in the main family view of your software. All other lower peerage titles are entered in the AKA title field along with the given name and the surname for each title.

- **Religious Titles**

Title Prefixes and Suffixes

The following charts show both the title prefixes and title suffixes for civil, military, religious, professional, peerage, and other titles of nobility. The prefix titles are optional for almost all titles; a few exceptions exist for religious titles, which are included below.

Civil Titles

All civil titles are entered as an event, as explained below. They are not entered into the Title Prefix or Title Suffix field of your software. Most civil titles are a result of holding office or high appointment and are entered using the Office event. Refer to the Office event tag on page 171 or the Occupation event tag on page 170. If using a paper FGR form, all civil titles are entered in the Notes field. The following civil titles are those most frequently used in family history research and are provided for your reference.

Table 3. Civil Titles

Civil Titles	Explanation
Administrator	
Alderman	Member of local legislative body, such as a town or city. Sometimes in England and Wales the title is given to the senior member of such a body.
Ambassador	A diplomatic official sent to represent one country to another.
Ambassador at large	A diplomatic official who represents one country but is not assigned to a specific country.
Assemblyman	A male member of a legislative assembly.
Assemblywoman	A female member of a legislative assembly.
Assistant Secretary of …	Example: Assistant Secretary of State.
Associate Justice of the Supreme Court of the USA	
Associate Justice of the Supreme Court of Canada	
Attorney General of … (followed by the municipal jurisdiction, such as city, county, state or country)	

Civil Titles, Continued

Bailiff	A feudal lord's manorial manager.
Burgess	An elected representative of a borough in Parliament.
Name of Cabinet Office	
Chief Justice of the Supreme Court of the USA	
Clerk of the House	
Clerk of the Senate	
Commissioner of ...	
Congressman from ... (followed by the jurisdiction)	
Consul	
Councilman	
Councilwoman	
Ealdorman	Old English spelling; use Alderman instead.
Governor of ... (followed by the jurisdiction)	
Governor General	

Civil Titles, Continued

Lieutenant Governor of …	
Lord Advocate	
Lord Chancellor	
Lord High Chancellor	
Lord High Chief Justice of …	
Member of the House of Commons	
Member of the House of Representatives of the State of …	
Member of the House of Representatives of the United States of America	
Lord Mayor of …	Use for Great Britain and Canada. For mayor in the U. S., see Mayor.
Lady Mayoress	Use for Great Britain and Canada.
Lord Master of the Rolls	
Lord Provost of …	Use for Great Britain and lower court of Canada.
Mayor of …	Use for Canada, England, and USA.

Civil Titles, Continued

Member of Parliament	
Member of Provincial Legislative Council	
Member of Provincial Legislature	
Minister of …	Use when assigned as minister to a foreign country.
Her Majesty's Minister for the United Kingdom	
President of the Senate of … (followed by the name of the state)	
President of the Senate of the United States	
33rd President of the United States of America	
Premier of the Province of …	
President of the Legislative Council	
Prime Minister of …	Use for Canada or the United Kingdom.

Civil Titles, Continued

Regent of …	
Senator from …	
Solicitor General	
Speaker of the … (followed by the name of the legislative body)	
Undersecretary of …	
Vice President of the United States	
Viceroy	For Viceroy use: Lord Lieutenant of Ireland or The Viceroy of India
Vice Chancellor	
Vice Consul	
Vizier	

Military Titles

Enter the military titles for officers in the Title Prefix and Title Suffix fields of your family history software as follows: Enter the military rank of an officer in the Title Prefix field. Then enter the name of the service that the officer belongs to in the Title Suffix field.

Nonofficer titles should be entered as military events. They should not be entered in the Title Prefix or Title Suffix field in your software.

All other military information should be recorded using the Military Event or the Notes field of your FGR. Please refer to the following tables for officer title prefixes and suffixes for military personnel. Refer also to Military event tag on page 168.

Table 4. Examples of Premodern Officer Military Titles

Title Prefix	Title Suffix
Admiral of the Blue	(None)
Admiral of the Red	(None) Forerunner of a modern Admiral
Admiral of the White	(None) Forerunner of a modern Vice Admiral
Brigadier General	(None)
Imperator	Roman General of … (followed by the name of the legion)

61

Table 5. United States Air Force—Modern Titles

Title Prefix	Title Suffix
General of the Air Force	United States Air Force
General	United States Air Force
Lieutenant General	United States Air Force
Major General	United States Air Force
Brigadier General	United States Air Force
Colonel	United States Air Force
Lieutenant Colonel	United States Air Force
Major	United States Air Force
Captain	United States Air Force
Lieutenant	United States Air Force
Second Lieutenant	United States Air Force

Table 6. United States Army—Modern Titles

Title Prefix	Title Suffix
General of the Army	United States Army
General	United States Army
Lieutenant General	United States Army
Major General	United States Army
Brigadier General	United States Army
Colonel	United States Army
Lieutenant Colonel	United States Army
Major	United States Army
Captain	United States Army
Lieutenant	United States Army
Second Lieutenant	United States Army

Table 7. United States Marine Corps—Modern Titles

Title Prefix	Title Suffix
General	United States Marine Corps
Lieutenant General	United States Marine Corps
Major General	United States Marine Corps
Brigadier General	United States Marine Corps
Colonel	United States Marine Corps
Lieutenant Colonel	United States Marine Corps
Major	United States Marine Corps
Captain	United States Marine Corps
Lieutenant	United States Marine Corps
Second Lieutenant	United States Marine Corps

Table 8. United States Navy—Modern Titles

Title Prefix	Title Suffix
Fleet Admiral	United States Navy
Admiral	United States Navy
Vice Admiral	United States Navy
Rear Admiral Upper Half	United States Navy
Rear Admiral Lower Half	United States Navy
Captain	United States Navy
Commander	United States Navy
Lieutenant Commander	United States Navy
Lieutenant Commander	United States Navy
Lieutenant Junior Grade	United States Navy
Ensign	United States Navy

Table 9. United Kingdom, Australia, and New Zealand Royal Air Force—Modern Titles

Title Prefix	Title Suffix
Marshal of the Royal Air Force	(None)
Air Chief Marshal	Royal Air Force
Air Marshal	Royal Air Force
Air Vice Marshal	Royal Air Force
Air Commodore	Royal Air Force
Group Captain	Royal Air Force
Wing Commander	Royal Air Force
Squadron Leader	Royal Air Force
Flight Lieutenant	Royal Air Force
Flying Officer	Royal Air Force
Pilot Officer	Royal Air Force

Table 10. United Kingdom, Australia, and New Zealand British Army—Modern Titles

Title Prefix	Title Suffix
Field Marshal	British Army
General	British Army
Lieutenant General	British Army
Major General	British Army
Brigadier	British Army
Colonel	British Army
Lieutenant Colonel	British Army
Major	British Army
Captain	British Army
Lieutenant	British Army
Second Lieutenant	British Army

Table 11. United Kingdom, Australia, and New Zealand Royal Marines—Modern Titles

Title Prefix	Title Suffix
General	Royal Marines
Lieutenant General	Royal Marines
Major General	Royal Marines
Brigadier	Royal Marines
Colonel	Royal Marines
Lieutenant Colonel	Royal Marines
Major	Royal Marines
Captain	Royal Marines
Lieutenant	Royal Marines
Second Lieutenant	Royal Marines

Table 12. United Kingdom, Australia, and New Zealand Royal Navy—Modern Titles

Title Prefix	Title Suffix
Admiral of the Fleet	Royal Navy
Admiral	Royal Navy
Vice Admiral	Royal Navy
Rear Admiral	Royal Navy
Commodore	Royal Navy
Captain	Royal Navy
Commander	Royal Navy
Lieutenant Commander	Royal Navy
Lieutenant	Royal Navy
Sub Lieutenant	Royal Navy
Midshipman	Royal Navy

Religious Titles

Religious titles that are held for life are entered in the Title Prefix and Title Suffix fields. Religious titles that are not held for life are entered using a Religion event tag. Refer to Religion event tag on page 175.

When using a religious title prefix or suffix, enter the title in the language your ancestor used or the language of your ancestor's country of origin.

The title prefix is optional, but if one is used, the first letter of each word in the title prefix is capitalized. If the title in the Title Suffix field is followed by a geographic location, the title is not capitalized (but the geographic location is).

Religious titles held by members of the Church of Jesus Christ of Latter-day Saints are not recorded with a title prefix or suffix when entering your ancestor's information. This title information is entered using a Religion event tag. Refer to Religion event tag on page 175.

Please refer to the following charts to locate religious title prefixes and suffixes. The religion and language of usage has been included in some instances. Explanations have been added to help clarify religious titles where necessary.

Examples of entering religious title prefixes (optional) and suffixes

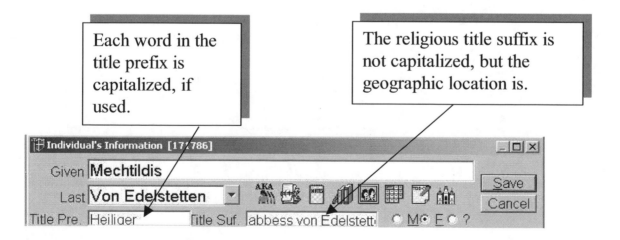

70

Table 13. Most Commonly Used Religious Titles in Family History Sources

Title Prefix	Title Suffix	Religion or Language	Explanation
(None)	Ab	Irish	An abbot.
(None)	Aba	Scottish-Gaelic	An abbot.
(None)	Abade	Portuguese	An abbot.
(None)	Abbas	Latin	An abbot.
(None)	Abbatatus	Latin	An abbot.
(None)	Abbé de or d'…	French	An abbot.
The Right Reverend	Abbot of …		The head monk in charge of an abbey or monastery.
(None)	Abbess of …		The head nun in charge of a convent.
(None)	Abesse de or d'…	French	An abbess.
(None)	Der abt	German	An abbot.
(None)	Ærkebiskop	Danish	An archbishop.
(None)	Antistes	Latin	A bishop.

(None)	Apostate		Someone who is no longer active in a Christian congregation. May also include those who have officially renounced previously held religious beliefs.
(None)	Apostle	Early Christian	One of the twelve disciples of Jesus Christ.
(None)	Apostolic delegate	Roman Catholic	An ambassador of the pope who is assigned to a country that does not have formal diplomatic relations with the Vatican.
The Most Reverend	Archbishop of …	Church of England	The head bishop who officiates over an archdiocese or ecclesiastical province.
His Eminence	Archbishop of …	Roman Catholic	The head bishop who officiates over an archdiocese or ecclesiastical province.
The Venerable	Archdeacon of …	Church of England	A member of the clergy who ranks just below a bishop and is usually his assistant.

(None)	Archevêque	French	An archbishop.
(None)	Ardeaspag	Irish	An archbishop.
(None)	Archidiacre	French	An archdeacon.
(None)	Archidiaconus	Latin	An archdeacon.
(None)	Archiepiscopus	Latin	An archbishop.
(None)	Archipresbyter	Latin	A chief priest in a collegiate church.
(None)	Arhat	Buddhism Sanskrit	A saint, monk or enlightened disciple who has reached the highest state.
(None)	Bischof	German	A bishop.
Lord	Bishop of …	Anglican	
Reverend	Bishop of …	Roman Catholic, Orthodox, Episcopal, Methodist	A senior cleric in charge of a diocese.
Reverend	Titular Bishop		Holds the title of bishop but is no longer officiating in the functions of that office.
(None)	Brahmin	Hinduism Sanskrit	A priest, of the highest social castes.

(None)	Caliph or Kalifa	Islam Arabic	A Muslim ruler who derives his religious authority to rule from descent from Muhammad.
Reverend	Canon of ... (followed by name of cathedral)		A clergyman who is assigned to a specific cathedral.
(None)	Cantarista	Latin	A priest.
(None)	Cantry	Latin	A priest.
His Eminence	Cardinal	Roman Catholic	Advisor to the pope, ranking just under the pope.
(None)	Catascopus	Latin	An archdeacon or bishop.
(None)	Chamberlain for ... (followed by the name of the pope)	Roman Catholic	A priest whose official duty is as a papal attendant.
(None)	Chaplain of ...		A member of the clergy who has pastoral duties for military personnel and prisons.
(None)	Chorepiscopus	Latin	A suffregan bishop.
(None)	Clergyman		A man who has been ordained for religious service in a Christian church.

(None)	Clergywoman		A woman who has been ordained for religious service in a Christian church.
Reverend	Clerk of …		
(None)	Cucullatus	Latin	A monk.
(None)	Curate		An assistant parish priest.
Reverend	Deacon	Anglican, Episcopalian	
(None)	Deacon	Roman Catholic, Orthodox	
Reverend	Dean of … (followed by the name of the cathedral)	Roman Catholic	In this case, the name of the cathedral is the location, so it is capitalized.
(None)	Diacinus or Diaconus	Latin	A deacon.
(None)	Diacre	French	A deacon.
Reverend	Diocesan of …		A bishop of a Diocese.
(None)	Doctor of Divinity (see explanation)		Do not enter as a title; instead, use the Education event tag.

(None)	Easpag	Irish	See bishop.
(None)	Elder of …		Senior lay member of a Christian church having the authority to act in some or all administrative duties.
(None)	Episcopus	Latin	A bishop.
(None)	Évêque de …	French	A bishop.
(None)	Exarch	Eastern Orthodox Church	A bishop.
Friar or Frère or Frater	(None)	Roman Catholic	A man who belongs to a religious order.
(None)	Godparents (see explanation)	Anglican and Roman Catholic	Do not enter as a title; instead, use the Religion event tag.
(None)	Guru	Sikhism	A spiritual leader.
(None)	Hajji	Islam	A Muslim who has completed pilgrimage to Mecca, Saudi Arabia.

(None)	Imam	Islam	A direct descendent of Muhammad, a prayer leader of a mosque, or a leader of an Islamic community.
(None)	Inclusa	Latin	A nun.
(None)	Inclusus	Latin	A monk.
His Excellency	Internuncio of … (followed by the name of the pope)	Roman Catholic	A representative of the pope.
(None)	Lohan	Buddhism	A saint, a monk, or an enlightened disciple.
(None)	Magi or Magus (Greek form) or Magu (Persian form)	Zoroastrianism	A priest of ancient Persia or a Zoroastrian priest.
(None)	Manach	Irish	See monk.
(None)	Minister	English	
(None)	Minister	Latin	See peerage titles for thane.
(None)	Ministre	French	A minister.
(None)	Ministro	Italian	A minister.
(None)	Moine	French	A monk or a friar.
(None)	Monaca	Italian	A nun.

77

(None)	Monacus or Monachus	Latin	A monk.
(None)	Monaco	Italian	A monk.
(None)	Monara, Monacha or Monialis	Latin	A nun.
(None)	Mönch	German	A monk.
(None)	Monja	Spanish	A nun.
(None)	Monje	Spanish	A monk.
(None)	Missionary		
(None)	Monk		
Reverend Mother Superior	Convent of …		
Reverend Mother	Convent of …		
(None)	Munk	Hungarian	A monk.
(None)	Munuc	Old English	
(None)	Nonne	French, German and Hungarian	A nun.
His Excellency	Nuncio for… (name of the pope)	Roman Catholic	A representative of the pope sent to a country that has diplomatic relations with the Vatican.

(None)	Nun	Roman Catholic	A woman who dedicates her life to religious service and devotion as a member of a community of women.
(None)	Obispo	Spanish	A bishop.
Padre	(None)	Roman Catholic Spanish	Priest of a Spanish-speaking church.
(None)	Pap	Hungarian	A priest.
Reverend	(None)		
Right Reverend Monsignor	Ablegate of His Holiness the Pope	Roman Catholic	Use for Papal Ablegate.
Right Reverend Monsignor	Papal Chamberlain	Roman Catholic	
His Excellency	Papal Nuncio	Roman Catholic	
(None)	Párroco	Spanish	A vicar.
Reverend	Parson of …		A clergyman or minister in charge of a parish.
(None)	Pastore	Italian	A minister.

(None)	Praest	Hungarian	A priest. For Roman Catholic priest, use katolsk praest.
Reverend	Pastor of …		A minister or a priest.
His Beatitude	Patriarch of …	Eastern Orthodox	
His Excellency	Patriarch of …	Roman Catholic	
Pope	(None)	Roman Catholic	
Very Reverend	Preacher	General	
Reverend	Preost	Old English for Priest	
(None)	Presbyter	Latin	A priest.
(None)	Priest	Roman Catholic, Anglican, Eastern Orthodox	
(None)	Priester	German	A priest.
Reverend Father Provincial	(Name of order)		
(None)	Presbyter	Latin	
(None)	Prieur	French	A prior.

Very Reverend Dom	Prior of …	Use for Claustral Prior	The head of a priory or other religious house in an abbey. The person second in authority below the abbot.
(None)	Prior of … (followed by initials of order)	Use for Conventual Prior	
(None)	Prioress of …		
(None)	Privy Chamberlain for … (followed by the name of the pope)	Roman Catholic	
(None)	Proctor or Procurator		A religious form of a solicitor or attorney used by many denomi-nations. If used as a nonreligious title, refer to Occupation event tag on page 170.
(None)	Prophet	Islam	
(None)	Prophet	Judiasm	
Very Reverend	Provost of … (followed by name of cathedral or university church)		The highest-ranking clergyman of a cathedral or university church.

(None)	Rakan	Buddhism	A saint, a monk, or an enlightened disciple.
Rabbi	(None)	Judaism	A teacher of doctrine.
(None)	Rebbes	Hasidic Judaism	A spiritual leader.
Very Reverend	Rector of … (followed by the name of the order)	Anglican	A clergyman who holds the rights and tithes of his parish.
Very Reverend	Rector of … (followed by the name of the order)	Episcopal	A minister in charge of a parish.
Very Reverend	Rector of … (followed by the name of the order)	Roman Catholic	The head priest of a parish.
(None)	Religieuse	French	A nun.
(None)	Religiosa	Italian	A nun.
Reverend	(None)		A title of respect for a clergyman, always used as title prefix.
Reverend Dom	Initials of order of Benedictine or Cistercian orders		
Venerable Father Dom	Initials of order of Carthusian orders		

Very Reverend Dom	Initials of order		Use for Claustral Prior.
(None)	Rialta	Irish	See Nun.
(None)	Roshi	Buddhism	A teacher of Zen Buddhism.
(None)	Sacerdote	Spanish	See Priest.
(None)	Sacerdozio	Italian	See Priest.
(None)	Sanctimonialis	Latin	A nun.
(None)	Sadhu		A Jain monk.
(None)	Sadhu Svetambara		A white-clad Jain monk.
(None)	Sagart	Irish	See Priest.
(None)	Samurai	Shinto	A religious warrior, similar to a knight in the crusades.
(None)	Sempectae	Latin	A senior monk of the Benedictine order.
(None)	Shogun	Shinto	A hereditary religious warrior leader, similar to a crusader.
(None)	Sika	Sikhism	A disciple.
Sister	Name of religious order	Roman Catholic	A female member of a religious order.

(None)	Sóknarprestur	Icelandic	A vicar.
Most Reverend Father	Superior General of the (enter the name of the order) Fathers	Roman Catholic	
Reverend Mother	Initials of the religious order, Superior General of …	Roman Catholic	The highest-ranking female member of a religious order.
(None)	Syr	Welsh	A cleric (often confused with sir marchog, which means sir knight).
Vénérer	(None)	French	A reverend.
(None)	Vescovo	Italian	A bishop.
Right Reverend	Vicar	Anglican	A priest of a parish who is not a rector.
Right Reverend	Vicar	Episcopal	A minister in charge of one chapel in a parish.
Right Reverend	Vicar	Roman Catholic	A priest acting as a deputy of a bishop.
Right Reverend Monsignor	Vicar General		The highest-ranking vicar.
(None)	Vicario	Spanish	See Vicar, Roman Catholic.
(None)	Vicarius or Vigerius	Latin	See Vicar, Roman Catholic.

Professional, Trade, Occupational, and Educational Titles

All professional, trade, and occupational titles are entered as an event in your software. They are not entered in the Title Prefix or Title Suffix field. Refer to the Occupation event tag on page 170. If using a paper FGR form, all professional, trade, and occupational titles are entered in the Notes field. The following professional, trade, and occupational titles are provided for your reference.

All scholastic titles should be entered as an education event if you are using a computer program. Refer to Education event tag on page 159. If using a paper FGR form, all scholastic titles are entered in the Notes field.

Table 14. Examples of Professional, Trade, Occupational, and Educational Titles

Attorney at Law	Director of …
Barrister	Grand Butler
Chamberlain of … (the manager of a household for a member of royalty or nobility)	Medical Doctor
Cupbearer	Veterinarian
Dean of University or College	Director of …
Dentist	Provost of … (followed by the name of a university or prison)

Peerage and Other Titles of Nobility

Title prefixes that are entered in the Title Prefix field are always capitalized for all nobility (titled aristocracy of a country), peerage (the rank or status of a nobleman or noblewoman), and royalty (king, queen, or other member of a monarch's family) regardless of country of origin. The title prefix is optional when entering peerage titles.

In the Title Suffix field, the name of the peerage or royal title is not capitalized but the name of the land governed is. This may be a state, province, region, country, or empire.

For both males and females, all details and notes regarding a peerage title are entered using a Title event. Refer to Title event tag on page 179.

For example, to enter His Royal Highness, William I "the Lion," king of Scotland, or His Grace, William IX Cavendish, duke of Devonshire, refer to the two examples below.

Examples of usage of peerage title prefixes and suffixes

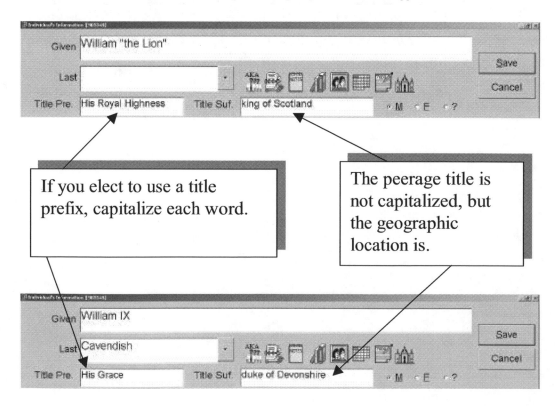

86

To clarify the order in which your ancestor held a peerage title, enter the number notation just before the title held (e.g., 3rd earl of March) only if it is given in your source documentation.

Example

Enter the number notation just before the peerage title.

Female Titles

Wives of a peer are accorded a peerage title only if any one of the following three conditions is met:

1. An original source refers to the wife by title.
2. Recorded dates indicate the wife was living and still married when her husband became a peer.
3. A source indicates the wife inherited a peerage title of her own.

Styled Titles

Styled means that the individual assumed the use of a title but never actually received that title. In such cases, the word "styled" is inserted in the Title Suffix field just prior to entering the title. The title is then entered in quotation marks.

Example of entering a styled title

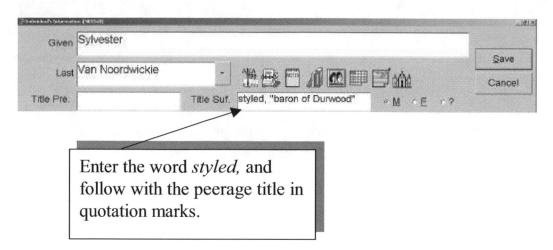

Enter the word *styled,* and
follow with the peerage title in
quotation marks.

Order When Entering Multiple Titles of Peerage

When recording an ancestor who had multiple peerage titles, enter the highest title held in the main Title Suffix field of your family view. All other titles are entered in the AKA field along with your ancestor's given name and surname. The following is an example of order of precedence:

- Emperor
- King
- Prince
- Duke
- Marquess or marquis
- Earl or count
- Viscount
- Baron or lord
- Baronet
- Knight
- Esquire

Each title is entered in the language spoken in the household of your ancestor at birth, or the language of his country of origin (e.g., duc de Normandie, graf von Heinenberg, earl of Derby, re de Espagne, conde di Coimbra, marquis di Saluzzo).

The geographic location over which your ancestor held the highest title is capitalized (e.g., Edward V, king of England). All other parts of the title are entered in lowercase (e.g., prince of Wales, duke of Cornwall, earl of Chester, earl of March, earl of Pembroke).

The date each title was acquired may also be entered as an event with details about the title. Refer to Title event tag on page 179.

Table 15. Commonly Used Peerage and Other Titles of Nobility and Royalty

Title Prefix	Title Suffix	Explanation
(None)	Abeto	An Ethiopian prince.
(None)	Akwamuhene	A ruler or tribal chieftain of the Akwamu found in Ghana.
(None)	Alafin	A ruler or tribal chieftain of the Oyo found in Nigeria.
(None)	Alaketu	A ruler or tribal chieftain of the Abeokuta found in Nigeria.
(None)	Amir of …, emir of …, ameer of …, and emeer of … are all acceptable. However, the most common usage is emir.	A prince or tribal chieftain in the Middle East.
His Grace	Archduke of …	All daughters are given the title prefix of Lady.
Her Grace	Archduchess of …	
(None)	Archiduc de … or Archiduc d'…	A French archduke.
(None)	Arkehertig	A Swedish archduke.
(None)	Asantehemaa	A title given to the Queen Mother of the Ashanti found in Ghana.
(None)	Asantehene	A title given to the king or tribal chieftain of the Ashanti found in Ghana.

(None)	Atheling	A title given to an Anglo-Saxon nobleman or prince who is usually heir to the throne.
(None)	Aula	The Latin form of court baron.
(None)	Atta	A title given to tribal chieftains of the Igala found in Nigeria.
(None)	Banbharún	The Irish form of baroness.
Sir	Banneret; use knight banneret of …	A knight who could lead his own men or a company of vassals under his banner into battle and has precedence in rank over other knights. The king or queen could also give out the title knight banneret for bravery.
(None)	Banphrionsa	The Irish form of princess.
(None)	Banríon	The Irish form of queen.
(None)	Baran	The Scottish-Gaelic form of baron.
(None)	Baro	The Latin form of baron.
Lord	Baron of …	The peerage title of baron is the lowest rank in higher British nobility. All daughters are given the title prefix of Lady.
(None)	Barón de …	The Spanish form of baron.
(None)	Baronatus	The Latin form of baronet.

Lady	Baroness of …	The wife of a baron.
(None)	Baronissa	The Latin form of baroness.
Sir	Baronet of …	The lowest British hereditary rank, below a baron but above a knight except for knights of the Garter. This title is not considered a peerage title and should not be entered in a title field; instead, use the Titles event tag to enter your ancestor's information. Wives are given the title prefix of Lady (Dame was formerly used for wife of a baronet).
(None)	Baronne de … or baronne d'…	The French form of baroness.
(None)	Barún	The Irish form of baron.
(None)	Beglerbeg	A title given to a ruler of a province in the Ottoman Empire.
(None)	Batonischvili	A Royal Prince of Georgia.
(None)	Begum	A title given to a princess in the East Indies; also a term used for Muslim women of high rank in India and Pakistan.
(None)	Bey	A title given to a ruler of the kingdom of Tunis.
(None)	Beyzade	A title given to the sons of a Sultan's daughters.

(None)	Bicas, Biceas, or Biocas	The Scottish-Gaelic form of viscount.
(None)	Bimbilla-na	A ruler or tribal chieftain of the Nanumba found in Ghana.
(None)	Boyar	A Russian nobleman prior to Peter the Great.
(None)	Burgrave of … or Burggraf von …	A German nobleman who rules a burg or castle.
Lady (Dame was formerly used for this title)	(None for a baronet's wife)	
(None)	Caliph of …	A title given to male Muslim rulers. Usually, the authority to rule is derived from a lineal descent from Muhammad. The term is used for both temporal and spiritual rulers. The sultans of Turkey also use this term.
(None)	Caesar	A title given to Roman emperors.
(None)	Cavallera de …	Spanish form of a female knight.
(None)	Cavallero de …	Spanish form of a male knight.
(None)	Cacique or Cazique	A chief in some Native Indian tribes of north and south America, especially of the West Indies and Latin America.
(None)	Chevaliere de … or chevaliere d'…	French form for a male knight.

(None)	Chevaleresses de … or chevaleresses d'…	French form of a female knight.
(None)	Chi Timukulu	A ruler or tribal chieftain of the Bemba found in Zambia.
(None)	Chief of … (followed by the name of the tribe or clan)	
(None)	Chieftain of … (followed by the name of the tribe or clan)	
(None)	Comte de … or comte d'…	The French form of earl or count.
(None)	Conde de	The Spanish form of earl or count.
(None)	Conte di	The Italian form of count.
Lord	Count of …	A count is a nobleman in multiple European countries ranking equally to an English earl. "Count of" should be translated into the language of your ancestor.
Lady	Countess of …	The wife of a count.
(None)	Contessa	An Italian countess.
(None)	Cunta	The Irish form of count.
(None)	Cuntaois	The Irish form of countess.
(None)	Czar of … (See Tzar)	
(None)	Czarowitz	The title given to the eldest son and heir to the Russian throne.

Dame	Followed by the order of knights or the husband's title if higher.	A Danish lady.
Dame of Grace	Followed by the order of knights.	
Dame of Justice	Followed by the order of knights.	
(None)	Dauphin de la France	A dauphin is a title given to the eldest son and heir to the French throne. Only the French form of the title should be used.
(None)	Dauphine de la France	A dauphine is the wife of a dauphin. Only the French form of the title should be used.
(None)	Denkyerahene	A ruler or tribal chieftain of the Denkyera found in Ghana.
(None)	Dey	A title given to the rulers of Tunis, Tripoli, and Algiers.
(None)	Dictator of …	An ancient Roman magistrate; also used in modern times as an absolute ruler.
(None)	Diúc	The Irish form of duke.
Domina	(None)	The Latin form of lady or dame.
(None)	Dronning or dronningen	A Danish or Norwegian queen.
(None)	Duc de … or duc d'…	The French form of duke.
(None)	Duca di …	An Italian duke.

(None)	Il duce	Italian form of leader.
His Grace	Duke of ...	The highest hereditary rank below that of a prince in English nobility. All daughters are given the title prefix of Lady.
His Royal Highness	Duke of ... (use if of royal blood)	All daughters are given the title prefix of Lady.
Her Grace	Duchess of ...	The wife of a duke.
Her Royal Highness	Duchess of ... (use if of royal blood)	
(None)	Duque	The Spanish form of duke.
(None)	Dux of ...	The Latin form of duke.
Lord	Earl of ...	The rank below a marquis and above a viscount in English nobility. All daughters are given the title prefix of Lady (for wife of an earl see Countess). The eldest son is given the title of viscount, all other sons use Honorable as a title prefix.
(None)	Elector of ...	
(None)	Emir	A prince or tribal chieftain in the Middle East.

(None)	Byzantine Emperor	
(None)	Emperor of ...	
(None)	Holy Roman Emperor	
(None)	Byzantine Empress	
(None)	Empress of ...	
(None)	Holy Roman Empress	
Sir	Eques	The Latin form of male knight.
(None)	Equitissa	The Latin form of female knight.
Master	Esquire, escuier, or ecutarius, also squire	An attendant and shield bearer for a knight, usually also a candidate for knighthood. Also used by those who had a commissioned office by the crown, such as a Justice of the Peace.
(None)	Franklin (do not use franklin or yeoman in title fields. Refer to Occupation event tag on page 170.)	A free tenant farmer in the feudal system.
(None)	Führer von ...	A German title given to a leader.
Master	Gentlemen (do not use in title fields. Refer to Title event tag on page 179.)	Below a baron and above a yeoman having no peerage. In England, was entitled to the use of a coat of arms.

(None)	Gentry (do not use in title fields.)	The term gentry is reserved for individuals who rank just below British nobility but who do not have hereditary rank or title.
(None)	Graf von …	A German count or earl.
(None)	Gräfin von …	A German countess.
(None)	Graffo	The Latin form of count, earl, or reeve.
His Grace or His Royal Highness (if of royal blood)	Grand duke of …	
Her Grace or Her Royal Highness (if of royal blood)	Grand duchess of …	
(None)	Grand master of …	
(None)	Greve	A Danish, Norwegian, or Swedish count.
(None)	Grevin'ne	A Norwegian countess.
(None)	Großherzg von …	A German grand duke.
(None)	Hajjaj of …	A Muslim ruler or governor.
Hanim	(None)	Turkish and Egyptain form of lady.

(None)	Heir von …	A German lord.
(None)	Hertig	A Swedish duke.
(None)	Hertug	A Danish or Norwegian duke.
(None)	Hertuginde	A Danish duchess.
(None)	Hertugin'ne	A Norwegian duchess.
(None)	Herzog von …	A German duke.
His Royal Highness	High king of …	
(None)	High steward of …	
(None)	Hospodar	A prince of Moldavia or Wallachia before they became Romania.
Hölgy	(None)	A Hungarian form of lady.
(None)	Husbandman (do not use in title fields. Refer to Occupation event tag on page 170.)	Husbandman is ranked below a franklin or yeoman and is a farmer of smaller plots of land while also working for larger farmers such as a yeoman.
(None)	Iarla	The Irish form of earl.
(None)	Imaum	A title given to a Mohammedan prince with direct lineal descent; also used by a priest who performs the regular services of a mosque.
Immabet-Hoy	(None)	Ethiopian form of lady.

(None)	Imperator (see Holy Roman Emperor or Military—Imperator)	
(None)	Inca	A ruler of the Quechuan peoples of Peru until the Spanish conquest.
(None)	Itege	Ethiopian form of empress.
(None)	Jarl of …	A nobleman or chieftain in Scandinavia.
(None)	Kabaka	A title given to kings of the Buganda found in Uganda.
(None)	Kahn	A title given to rulers of Mongols, Tartar, and some Turkish tribes.
(None)	Kaiser von	A title given to an emperor of the Holy Roman Empire, Austria, or Germany.
(None)	Khedive	A title given to Turkish viceroys who ruled Egypt after 1867.
His Royal Highness	King of …	
(None)	Király	A Hungarian king.
(None)	Királynö	A Hungarian queen.
Sir	Knight, followed by the order, then by the rank if given.	A nonhereditary rank below a baronet. The word "knight" should not be capitalized in the Title Suffix field.

(None)	Konge	A Danish or Norwegian king.
(None)	König von …	A German king.
(None)	Königin von …	A German queen.
(None)	Kung	A Swedish king.
(None)	Laird	The equivalent of a lord in Scotland but usually also a wealthy landowner.
(None)	Lamido	A title given to the Emirs of the Adamawa found in Nigeria.
(None)	Leelt Ras	Ethiopian form of Princess.
(None)	Leul Ras	Ethiopian form of Prince.
Lij	(None)	Ethiopian prefix title given to children of royal blood.
(None)	Litunga	A ruler or tribal chieftain of the Lozi found in Zambia.
(None)	Lord of …	Usually used as a form of address for an earl, marquis, or viscount. It is also used as a courtesy title for a son of a duke or marquis. A wife is given the title prefix of Lady.
His Excellency	Maharajah of …	An Indian prince ranked just above a rajah.

(None)	Maharani	A wife of a Maharajah.
(None)	Mai Bedde	A title given to the Emirs of Bedde found in Nigeria.
(None)	Mandarin	A title given to a Chinese nobleman or high-ranking government official.
(None)	Manikongo	A title given to the king or tribal chieftains found in the Congo.
(None)	Mar of …	
Sir (often confused with Syr, a Welsh cleric.)	Marchog of …	The Welsh form of knight.
(None)	Margrave von …	German equivalent of a marquess, ranking above a count, the lord chief justice of the March border or border area.
(None)	Markgrave	The Dutch form of marquess, meaning border count .
Lord	Marquess of …	The title given only to the eldest son of a duke. A marquess ranks between a duke and an earl in the United Kingdom. All daughters are given the title prefix of Lady.
Lady	Marchioness de … or marchioness d'…	The wife of a marquess.

Lord	Marquis of …	In continental European countries, a nobleman ranking above a count. All daughters are given the title prefix of Lady.
(None)	Master of …	
Maulay	Prince of Morocco	Maulay is a form of Lord given to all Princes of Morocco. It is used as a prefix title.
	Mek	A title given to rulers and tribal chieftains of the Tegale found in Sudan.
(None)	Mikado	A title given to hereditary rulers of Japan.
Sir	Miles	Latin form of knight.
Dame	Militissa	Italian form of female knight.
(None)	Mirza	Iranian form of Prince.
(None)	Moirear, mormaer, morhair, and murmor	The Scottish-Gaelic form of lord.
(None)	Mugabe	A title given to the kings of Ankole found in Uganda.
(None)	Mukama	A title given to many different rulers and kings in Uganda.
(None)	Mulopwe	A title given to many different rulers or tribal chieftains in Zaire.

(None)	Nabob or Nawab	An under-king of the Mogul Empire.
(None)	Ndlovukazi	Queen mother of Swaziland.
(None)	Negusa Nagast	Ethopian form of Emperor.
(None)	Ngwenyama	A title given to the kings of Swaziland.
(None)	Nizam	A ruler of the Hyderabad in India.
(None)	Nobleman (do not use in the title field.)	An individual who has hereditary rank or title. Usually refers to a baron.
(None)	Padishah	A title that used to be given to the ruling monarch of Iran, the sultan of Turkey, and the shah of Persia.
Pasha	(None)	Turkish form of Lord.
(None)	Patrician	A Roman aristocrat. Also a Byzantine title bestowed by the emperor for great service to the empire. A patrician had special privileges to nonhereditary offices and related privileges.
(None)	Pfalzgraf, palsgrave, or palatine	A feudal lord in Germany, usually a count or earl who had superintendence for a German royal house.
(None)	Potestas	Latin, used to refer to a king, chief, or ruler.

His Royal Highness	Prince of …	A nonreigning son of a royal family, ranking just below a king.
(None)	Princesa de …	The Spanish form of princess.
Her Royal Highness	Princess of …	A nonreigning daughter of a king, the wife of a prince, or the wife of a son of a prince.
(None)	Príncipe de …	A Spanish or Italian prince. The Italian form has no accent over the letter I.
(None)	Principe ereditario	An Italian prince royal.
(None)	Principessa	An Italian princess.
(None)	Prins	A Danish or Swedish prince.
(None)	Prinsesse	A Danish or Swedish princess.
(None)	Prinz von …	A German prince.
(None)	Prinzessin von …	A German princess.
(None)	Prìonnsa	The Scottish-Gaelic form of prince.
Her Royal Highness or Her Gracious Majesty	Queen of …	
His Royal Highness	Rajah of …	A Hindu king or prince in India or the East Indies.

(None)	Rani or Ranee	The wife of a rajah, or a princess or queen of India or the East Indies.
(None)	Re	An Italian king.
(None)	Regina	An Italian queen.
His Excellency	Regnant of …	
(None)	Reine de … or reine d'…	The French form of queen.
(None)	Rey de …	The Spanish form of king.
(None)	Reina de …	The Spanish form of queen.
(None)	Reth	A title given to rulers or tribal chieftains of the Shilluk found in Sudan.
(None)	Rìbhinn	The Scottish-Gaelic form of queen.
Sir	Ridder	A Danish knight.
Sir	Ridire	The Irish form of knight.
(None)	Rìgh	The Scottish-Gaelic form of king.
Sir	Ritter	A German knight.
(None)	Roi de … or roi d'…	The French form of king.
(None)	Sachem	A chief of a Native American tribe.

(None)	Sagamore	A subordinate tribal chief among the Algonquian Indians of North America.
(None)	Sarkin Dabai	A title given to the tribal chieftains of the Zuru found in Nigeria.
(None)	Sarkin Daura	A title given to the tribal chieftains of the Daura found in Nigeria.
(None)	Sarkin Kebbi	A title given to the tribal chieftains of the Kebbi found in Nigeria.
(None)	Sarkin Zazzau	A title given to the tribal chieftains of the Zaria found in Nigeria.
(None)	Satrap	A provincial ruler of Persia.
(None)	Sayyid	A title given to the male descendants of the Prophet Muhammad.
(None)	Sayyida	A title given to the female descendants of the Prophet Muhammad.
(None)	Seigneur de … or seigneur d'…	The French form of lord.
His Royal Highness	Shah of …	A hereditary monarch of a Middle Eastern country; most commonly used in Persia, which is now Iran.

His Royal Highness	Shahanshah of ...	A high king of a Middle Eastern country; most commonly used in Persia, which is now Iran.
(None)	Sharif	A title given to the male descendants of the Prophet Muhammad.
(None)	Sharifa	A title given to the female descendants of the Prophet Muhammad.
(None)	Sheik	The ruler of an Arab family, clan, tribe, or village.
(None)	Squire	The son of a knight.
(None)	Soldan	The sultan of Egypt, sometimes used synonymously with the term sultan.
(None)	Sultan or Grand Turk	A monarch of the Ottoman Empire or a Muslim country.
(None)	Suria	A title given to a second or lesser wife or mistress.
(None)	Tegnio, teignus, thainus, thaynus, or thingus	The Latin forms of thane.
(None)	Tetrarch	One of four joint rulers of the Roman Empire. Also used to refer to one of four provincial rulers of the Roman Empire.

(None)	Thane of ...	In Scotland, the equivalent of a baron. In England, a low ranking nobleman who promised military service to a lord in return for land.
(None)	Tiarna	The Irish form of lord.
(None)	Tsar or czar	The equivalent of an emperor; used in Russia before the 1917 revolution.
(None)	Tsarina, tsaritsa, czarina, or czaritza	The equivalent of an empress; used in Russia before the 1917 revolution.
(None)	Tycoon	A ruling Japanese shogun.
Right Honorable	Viscount of ...	A rank just below an earl or a count and just above a baron. All daughters are given the title prefix of Lady.
Lady	Viscountess of ...	The wife of a viscount.
His Excellency	Under-king of ...	
(None)	Zar or zarina	

C. Gender

Each record entered into your family history software must show the gender of that ancestor. Usually, you are given three choices: male, female, and unknown. Unknown is used when you cannot determine the gender because:

- The given name is not available.
- The gender cannot be determined from the given name recorded.
- A child died unnamed.

Example

Select the correct gender for your ancestor: male, female, or unknown, which is shown as a question mark in this software program.

If you are using a paper FGR form, it is unnecessary to identify the gender of parents since men are listed as husbands and women as wives.

To identify the children's gender on a paper FGR form, enter the gender of all children using "F" for females and "M" for males in the small box just to the left of their names.

If the gender is unknown, enter a "U" in the small box just to the left of their names. This may be necessary if you cannot read the first name, or if the name could be used by either a boy or girl. If your ancestor changed their gender, enter your ancestor's gender as it appeared on their original birth or baptismal certificate.

D. Events

Each event in your ancestor's life consists of a date and time, a geographic location, and an activity (event). This section describes in detail how to enter dates, geographic locations, and specific events. Also described are the standard set of event types used in family history. See Event Tags on page 149.

Dates

You can enter dates in many formats, but when you are finished the date will be converted to one of five predefined formats in your software (e.g., dd/mmm/yyyy, mmm/dd/yyyy, and European formats.) Usually, you must select your preference in the Options or Setup section of your program.

The most used format for genealogical research is the dd/mmm/yyyy format. This format is the most readable and least likely to create confusion when entering and utilizing the data. Abbreviate the names of months—using three characters only, with no ending period—as Jan, Feb, Mar, Apr, May, Jun, Jul, Aug, Sep, Oct, Nov and Dec.

Example

Enter the day first, followed by the month abbreviation, then the four-digit year.

Always enter a date for the birth of an individual even if you have to estimate it. Refer to Using About and Circa on page 118. By doing so, it will be easier to do further research on your ancestor and use the features of your software.

111

When You Do Not Have the Death Date

Occasionally, sources indicate only the demise of your ancestor but do not reveal the actual date. If you are unable to locate the date with further research, you may enter one of the following in the death date field of your family history software or a paper FGR form:

- If you desire to submit an individual for temple ordinances or wish to record the death of an indivudual, and you are sure an individual is dead but do not know the date of death and it is within 110 years of today's date, enter "Deceased" in the Death Date field.

- If a child died before the age of 3, enter the word "Infant" in the Death Date field.

- If the child died between the age of 3 and before the age of 8, enter the word "Child" in the Date field. This entry is also used when your source document does not clarify the age at the time of death but indicates the individual died as a child.

- In all other cases of missing death date information, the death date field is left blank.

Most family history software also has a field where you can indicate if your ancestor is living or deceased. Deceased should be indicated in all cases when you do not have a death date.

Example

Individual's Information [172676]

Given Susan Marie
Last Sullivan
Title Pre.   Title Suf.
Born 8 Jan 2000   in
Chr.   in
Died Infant   in
Bur.   in
User ID#   AFN

The word Deceased, Infant, or Child are permissible entries in the death date field.

112

A.D., C.E., B.C., B.C.E., and A.H. Dates

If you are using a computer program to enter your vital records, you should be able to enter both B.C. (before Christ) and A.D. (Anno Domini, or "in the year of our Lord") date suffixes. When using software that allows these B.C. and A.D. suffixes, use one space between the year and the abbreviation but no space between the letters (example: 34 B.C.).

Only a few programs allow the use of B.C., C.E. (common era or Christian era), and B.C.E. (before the common era) date suffixes after a given year. In most software programs it is not necessary to enter A.D. or C.E. date suffixes after a year in the common era. If you are using software that allows B.C., C.E., and B.C.E. date suffixes, you must enter these abbreviations with a space between the year and the suffix, and no space between the letters (example: 34 B.C.).

Example:

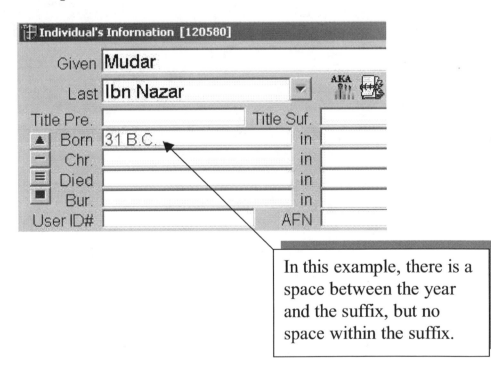

In this example, there is a space between the year and the suffix, but no space within the suffix.

A.H. is used only after dates entered using the Hijri Calendar. Refer to Other Calendars on page 130.

From and *To* Dates

"From" and "to" are used if entering a range of dates that runs from a starting date through an ending date. Although some software programs allow the use of hyphens when entering a range of dates, most do not, neither do they handle the import and export of these dates properly. To correctly enter a range of dates enter the word "From" followed by the beginning date, then the word "to" followed by the second or ending date.

Example

Your ancestor Senator Thomas Armstrong held office as an Assemblyman from 1827 to 1829.

Edit Event for Senator, Thomas Armstrong-[734]

Event: Office
Description: Assemblyman New York St
Date: From 1827 to 1829
Place: Lyons, Wayne County, New Yo

Notes   Sentence Override

Using *Before* and *After*

When you know that a specific event, such as a marriage, took place on a given date, you can derive "before" and "after" dates for other events, such as birth and death. The use of "before" and "after" is more desirable than guessing the actual birth and death dates when no other records are available.

Some software programs allow you to use the entire words "Before" and "After". Others abbreviate them to "Bef" and "Aft". Both forms are acceptable and can be mixed. In other words, you are allowed to use both the abbreviated version (for example, Bef) and the entire word (for example, After) in the same record.

114

Example of using before and after dates

You can document that your ancestor fought in a feudal tournament on 6 May 1529 in honor of his village and survived, and on June of 1577 went to live in a monastery. From these two events you can derive a "before" birth date and an "after" death date if you have no other information.

The birth date can be entered as Bef 6 May 1529.

The death date can be entered as After Jun 1577.

Next, enter documentation in the Source field for each date you have entered, and indicate that you derived the birth and death dates from these known dates. Finally, create an event using the Living event tag or in the Notes field of a paper FGR form for the known dates that your ancestor was alive. Refer to Living event tag on page 165.

Dates may also be derived from probate records that use "before" and "after".

Do not use "ante" or "post" in the date field.

Example

Your ancestor dated a will July 11, 1746 and it was proved December 15, 1749. You have four dates to enter from this information (approximate date of death, approximate date of burial, date the will was signed, and date the will was proved). Enter the death date as "After 11 Jul 1746". Then, enter the burial date as "Bef 15 Dec 1749". Enter the dates that the will was signed and later proved as events.

Finally, note in the Source field for each event the source of the dates that you do have, and that you derived the death and burial dates from these probate records.

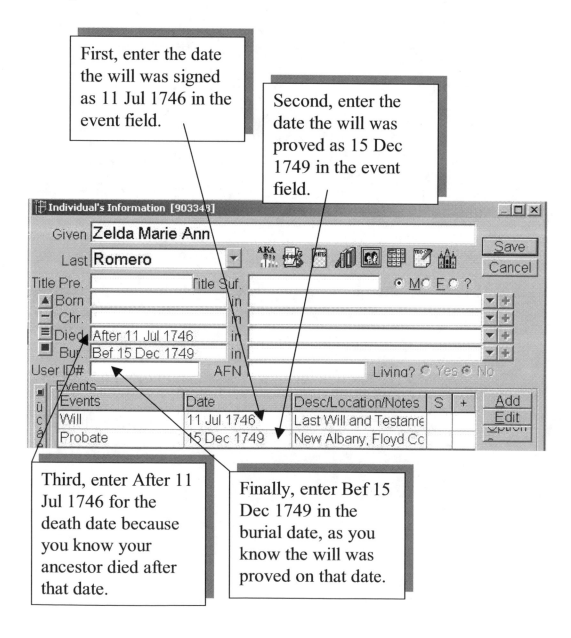

First, enter the date the will was signed as 11 Jul 1746 in the event field.

Second, enter the date the will was proved as 15 Dec 1749 in the event field.

Third, enter After 11 Jul 1746 for the death date because you know your ancestor died after that date.

Finally, enter Bef 15 Dec 1749 in the burial date, as you know the will was proved on that date.

Using Calculated Dates

Calculate unknown dates if possible. For example, if the age of an individual is known and documented at a given event, and the birth date is unknown, you may calculate the birth date from the date of the known event. You may also derive a birth date from a tombstone or death certificate. The calculated date should always be prefaced with the abbreviation "Cal"; for example:

Cal 4 Sep 1832

All dates that you have calculated based on another known date or age information given in the same source document should be prefaced with "Cal", and followed by the date. The source document should then be noted in your Source field with any additional explanation that might be necessary to make your entry as clear as possible to someone else who may rely on your data in the future.

Example

You identify from a tombstone inscription that your ancestor died 30 August 1777, at 73 years, 3 months, and 26 days old. The birth date you would enter is 4 May 1704. But you need to document that you calculated the date from another source. The correct entry is therefore "Cal 4 May 1704". This allows others with whom you share your research to know that this date was calculated from another date and is therefore better information than an estimated or guessed date. To complete the entry, you would indicate the source of the date you do have and that you calculated the date entered from that source.

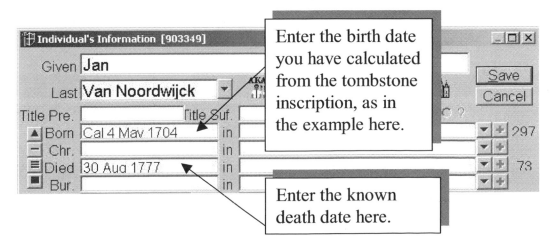

117

Using *About* or *Circa*

About is used when you do not know the exact date an event took place but you do know with some degree of certainty that the event occurred within a certain period of months or years. Use "Abt" (no period) as the abbreviation for about. "Abt" is used in front of the date. Do not use <date> to indicate an approximated date; dates surrounded by angle brackets are generated by your family history software when estimating dates and do not suggest any degree of likelihood that the information is accurate.

To use "Abt" before a date means you are providing your best guess, evaluation, or judgment in a situation where you currently have incomplete or inconsistent data. The about entry should be updated when you have more reliable data on which to base your calculations, and ultimately replaced with an exact date based on a documented source when you find one.

All individuals in your database should have an actual birth or death date, or, minimally, an approximated birth date. This will allow searching and other features of your software to work properly, thus helping to make further research easier.

If you must approximate a birth date for your ancestor, you may do any of the following:

- A birth date may be approximated from a marriage date. It is standard to approximate male births as being twenty-five years before a marriage date, and females twenty-one years before. Similarly, a first child's birth may be approximated as being a year after the marriage date. All other children are approximated in order of birth in two-year intervals.

- A birth date may be approximated from a baptismal date. The baptismal date is entered in the christening field, and then the approximated birth date is entered in the Birth field. It is standard to approximate a birth date as being *within* twelve months before the baptismal date for a child. If you aware of family, religious (where the denomination waits until a child is

118

eight or adult), or country practices, you may take those customs into consideration when approximating.

- A marriage date may be approximated from a documented birth date of your ancestor, or a documented birth date of the firstborn child of your ancestor. It is standard to approximate male first marriages as being twenty-five years after a birth date and females as being twenty-one years after. The marriage date may also be approximated as being a year before a first child's birth date.

Examples

Example 1: You know your ancestor was baptized 12 Sept 1768 according to the records of a Dutch Reformed church in Brooklyn, New York, and you know that your ancestor lived in Somerset, New Jersey, in a new Dutch settlement that did not have a church at that time. You know it would take some time to travel from the settlement to Brooklyn to perform the baptism. In this case you could enter the birth date as:

Abt 1768

Next, document the baptismal date and location in the baptism fields.

Example 2: If the baptism occurred 5 Jan 1768, your entry for the birth date should be:

Abt 1767 or 1768

You would not indicate the month of January because you have no indication that the birth took place in this month and to do so would be misleading to those with whom you share your information. Some software programs will list the date as Abt 1767/1768, using a virgule, or slash, between the two years.

ⓘ "Circa" is no longer used when entering genealogical data. Circa is a Latin term found in older genealogical research items that means the information was approximated. It was used interchangeably with "about" in modern usage. It was usually abbreviated in family history as Cir (e.g. Cir 5 Jan 1768) or using a tilda (e.g. ~1768). These circa entries should be converted to read Abt 5 Jan 1768 and Abt 1768, respectively.

Using *Between*

"Between" is useful when entering a date that took place between two other known events. Either "Between" or "Bet" may be entered before the first date, with the word "and" between the two dates.

Example

A bible entry for Fatima says she was the second child born between Alfred, who was born 19 May 1779, and Jacob, who was born 11 Nov 1806, but no date for her birth was given. Your entry would be as follows:

Enter the birth date as Between 19 May 1779 and 11 Nov 1806. Note: You will not be able to read your entire entry until you print out an FGR or a report, as your data is longer than your input window.

Entering a Season

On occasion, you will want to enter the season of year that you know an event happened, but you lack the exact day and, especially, the month. The following entries show the format recognized by most family history software as seasons, which will allow you to create standard GEDCOM files that can be shared with others:

- For spring of 1850, use: Between Mar 1850 and May 1850
- For summer of 1850, use: Between Jun 1850 and Aug 1850
- For fall of 1850, use: Between Sep 1850 and Nov 1850
- For winter of 1850, use: Between Dec 1850 and Feb 1851

Example of entering a season for a date

If your ancestor were born in the spring of 1802, your entry would appear as follows:

The season is entered in the date field: Enter the birth date as Between Mar 1802 and May 1802. You will not be able to view your entire entry until it is printed out in a report or chart.

Entering Incomplete Dates

Dates are usually entered using the dd/mmm/yyyy format. Frequently, dates are not recorded on tombstones or other historical documents in their entirety. Occasionally, you can read only a portion of the original document because of aging, handwriting, or damage. In these cases you can indicate the dates as follows:

When Only a Year Is Given

Frequently, a vital record will list only the year of a recorded event. When you find that this has happened, enter the year in your date field and cite your source in the Notes field. This will tell anyone accessing your file that this is a reliable date based on a reliable source, even though the date is incomplete.

Example

You have found a tombstone for your Uncle Howard indicating a birth date of 1895 and a death date of 1966. You would enter this information as follows:

Missing Day of Month

Frequently, a vital record is not totally legible. If you find yourself unable to read the name of the day that an event took place, you can omit the day and enter only the month and year.

Example

Next to your Uncle Howard's tombstone, you discover your Aunt Phoebe's tombstone, but it is very worn and you cannot read her birth date. However, you can still read the birth month and year as September 1888, and her death date as 18 July 1971.

You would enter "Sep 1888" in the birth date field and "18 Jul 1971" in the death date field. Then, in the Notes field for each event you would enter your source of information. In this case, you would also describe the condition of the tombstone to explain the missing information utilizing a Birth event tag. Refer to Birth event tag on page 153.

Note: If using a paper FGR form, the procedure is slightly different. You would leave two blank spaces for the unknown day, followed by the month and year as illustrated:

__ Sept 1888

Missing Month

When the month is missing, list only the year (e.g., 1924) and make a notation in your Notes field for the day of the month and why the month is not available or readable. Putting the day in the Notes field will avoid any possible confusion between the day and the month. Next, describe the condition of the document in your Source field after the citation of your source.

Example

Next to the tombstones of Howard and Phoebe you discover the badly damaged tombstone of a baby girl, Mildred. You can read the day of her death as the 19th and the year as 1924, but the month is totally illegible. Your entry would be as follows:

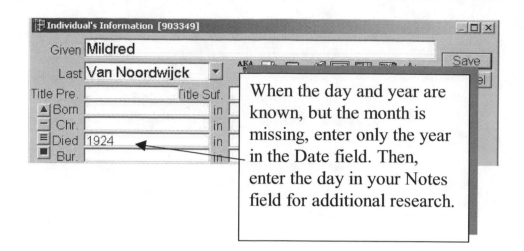

When the day and year are known, but the month is missing, enter only the year in the Date field. Then, enter the day in your Notes field for additional research.

Missing Year

If the year is missing and you are using family history software, list only the day followed by the month, leaving the year blank:

22 Sep

Make a notation in your Notes field documenting the source of the day and the month. Then explain the reason you cannot provide the year. In your Source field, after the citation of your source, describe the condition of the document.

There is a slightly different procedure for entering a missing year when using a paper FGR form. After you list the day and month, enter four underlined spaces for the missing year. This lets the reader know you did not accidentally forget to enter the year from the source that you were using.

22 Sept ____

Marriage Dates and Order

A FGR should be prepared for each married couple. Most software programs make a new FGR automatically for each marriage an individual has entered into.

If you are using a paper FGR form, you will have to make one sheet for each married pair manually. You can keep track of multiple marriages on paper FGR forms by prefixing each marriage partner with a number, which corresponds to the order in which each spouse was married.

Example

(1) Nancy Wilson, (2) Ann McDonald, (3) Susan Rita Adams

Also place an X in the See Other Marriages box on the paper FGR form.

Alternate Marriage Dates

Sometimes the exact date of a marriage is unknown, but what is known is the date the bride and groom obtained their marriage license, posted their banns of marriage, or announced their intent to marry. These dates may be entered into the marriage date field if you are sure your ancestors were married. Be sure to document what kind of alternate date you are using for the marriage date. Family history software allows you to use the prefix "Banns" or "Lic" if deriving the alternate date from posted marriage banns or a marriage license.

Example of entering the date of Banns instead of marriage date

Dispensation and settlement dates may also be used as alternate dates for a marriage date, although they are entered differently. The date for a dispensation or marriage contract is entered as "Abt" followed by the date. Next, the date of the dispensation or marriage contract is documented in the Source and Notes fields.

If you are entering alternate dates such as banns, license, or intention dates to document a marriage on a paper FGR form, use this format:

- **Banns 21 Nov 1798**
- **Lic 28 Aug 1870**
- **Int 11 Jan 1679**
- **Abt 22 Jul 1455** (for dispensations, settlements and other marriage contracts)

Divorce Dates

The procedure for entering divorce dates is different when entering the date in family history software versus entering the date on a paper FGR form.

If a divorce occurs, indicate it on paper versions in the Other Marriages section of the FGR form, being sure to include the date and place of the divorce. The date is preceded by "Div", the abbreviation for divorce, and followed by the place where the event took place:

Div 31 Apr 1977, Rochester, Monroe, New York, USA

On the family view of most family history software programs, there is a place to enter marriage information. In software, it is not necessary to enter the abbreviation for divorce before the date, as the data for marriage and divorce are recorded in separate fields.

Example of entering a divorce date

Your ancestor was married on 9 July 1548 and was divorced 28 January 1562. You would enter the marriage date in the marriage date field. Then you would select the status of "Divorce," then enter the divorce date in the status date field.

Marriage Information [MRIN: 2087]	_ □ ×
Hans Jacobson-[172676] & Jacomina Christjansen-[172678]	Save / Cancel

☐ This Couple Had No Children

Marr Date 9 Jul 1548 in Overyssel, Drenthe, Holland ▼

Ending Status Divorce ▼ Status Date (optional) 28 Jan 1562

Other Dating Systems

Feast Days

Religious calendars and cultural feasts do not always correspond with dates in the Julian or Gregorian calendars. Some events are recorded referring to a particular feast or Saint's day rather than the day and month. To enter these dates, see the following:

Example

The Lord of Halverson was buried the Thursday after All Saints Day 1428. This date would be entered only as "1428" in the date field and a note would be entered in the Notes field for the event indicating he was buried Thursday after All Saints Day 1428. If you refer to a conversion calendar and calculate the actual date, you would enter "Cal" before the calculated date. Refer to Using Calculated Dates on page 117.

Gregorian and Julian Calendar Dates

As early as 1582, many European countries using the Julian calendar began switching their method of dating to other calendars.

Beginning in 1752 and ending as late as 1923, nearly all countries not already using the Gregorian calendar switched to the Gregorian calendar introduced by Pope Gregory XIII.

You may find as a result of this change that events in your ancestor's life may have been recorded using a dual or double dating system for certain months in order to avoid confusion as countries made the calendar conversion.

All dates from the 25th of March through the 31st of December use a single dating system. All dates from the 1st of January through the 24th of March use the double dating system. Finally, all dates from the 25th of March return to the single dating system. The beginning year depends on the year each country officially adopted the Gregorian calendar.

Table 16. Julian/Gregorian Conversion Table Using Example Dates

Julian	Gregorian	Double
December 15, 1628	December 15, 1628	December 15, 1628
January 1, 1628	January 1, 1629	January 1, 1628/29
March 24, 1628	March 24, 1629	March 24, 1628/29
March 25, 1629	March 25, 1629	March 25, 1629

Quaker Dates

The Quaker dating system avoids the use of the names of the months and days. Instead the date is given as 1st month, 2nd month, and 1st day, 2nd day, etc. Prior to March 1753, the Julian calendar was used and "1st month" meant the month of March. After the adoption of the Gregorian calendar in March 1753, the "1st month" refers to January.

Quaker dates should be converted to the Gregorian calendar dates and entered with the abbreviation for calculated "Cal" before the date, and then the actual Quaker date should be entered in the Notes field for the date being recorded.

Quaker Date Conversions		
Julian Dates (Before 1753 the calendar year began March 1st)	**Quaker Month**	**Gregorian Dates** (After January 1, 1753)
March	1st Month	January
April	2nd Month	February
May	3rd Month	March
June	4th Month	April
July	5th Month	May
August	6th Month	June
September	7th month	July
October	8th Month	August
November	9th Month	September
December	10th Month	October
January	11th month	November
February	12th month	December

Other Calendars

Many calendars have been developed over thousands of years, some based on lunar events, some on solar and others (called lunisolar) are based on both. The Babylonian, Aztec, Zoroastrian, Egyptian, Greek, Roman, Hebrew, Mayan, Hindu, Inca, and Chinese are just some civilizations that have significant differences from the Julian or Gregorian calendars. Some calendars differ from the Gregorian calendar in the following ways: different starting points, different names for months and days, or a different number of days in a calendar year. Examples are the French Republic Calendar or the Hebrew Calendar.

Different calendars may range from 304 to 365 days per year. A few calendars begin their years counting from the year of creation. The Hijri calendar dates from 16 Jul 622 when the prophet Muhammad went from Mecca to Medina. If you are entering dates from the Hijri calendar, "A.H." is entered after the date where you would normally find A.D. or B.C. date suffixes.

Table 17 lists the Gregorian date of 18 September 2001 using several other calendar systems. You can convert all dates to the Gregorian calendar, or enter the dates using the calendar your ancestor used.[5]

Table 17. Examples of Calendar Date Formats

Calendar	Style to Use in Date Field
Gregorian	18 September 2001
Hebrew	28 Elul 5761
Hijri	27 Jumada t-Tania 1422
Persian	25 Shahrivar 1380
Mayan Long Count	12.19.8.10.6
Indian Civil	25 Bhadra 1923

---

[5] The current release of TempleReady will not process dates that have not been converted into the Gregorian dates; future versions will allow the use of alternate dating systems.

If you choose to convert your calendar dates, the following web sites and software may be helpful:

- Jewish dates—
  http://www.jewishgen.org/jos/josdates.htm

- Hijri Dates—http://www.cs.pitt.edu/~tawfig/convert/

- For a one-stop web site that offers freeware to convert any date to or from any of the following calendars: Gregorian, Julian, Julian Day, Hebrew, Hijri, Persian, Mayan, Baha'i, Indian Civil, and French Republican— http://www.fourmilab.ch/documents/calendar/

- Chinese calendar converter— http://www.mandarintools.com/calconv.html

- Universal Date Calculator (converts dates of 34 calendars, including most western calendars and others such as Hebrew, Hijri, Jelali, Yezdesred, Zoroastrian, Fasli, Armenian, Phoenician, Babylonian, Chaldean, Chinese, Thai Suriyakati, Thai Chantarakati, Seleucid, Macedonian, Coptic, Ethiopian, and several others used for shorter periods of time)— http://www.cf-software.com/ucc.htm

Regnal Dates

Ancient historical events and events that occurred during a feudal period may have been recorded with reference to the reign of a specific monarch. Regnal years begin with the first day the monarch began to reign and end with the monarch's death.

For example, Bernice de Montgomery died 27 Dec 1 Eliz.

This would mean that your ancestor Bernice died on the 27th of December during the first year of Queen Elizabeth's reign.

If you know that Queen Elizabeth reigned from 17 Nov 1558 to 24 Mar 1603, then you can then manually calculate that your ancestor died 27 Dec 1558 and the death date can be entered as "Cal 27 Dec 1558".

When you do not know the exact years a monarch ruled, enter the regnal year in the date field.[6]

Frequently historians and archeologists will disagree on the exact ancient regnal dates for monarchs. When this happens, it may be impossible to calculate the date based on the monarch's regnal years. If this is the case, leave the date field blank. Then enter, for example, "12th year of Ramses III", as the first item in the place name field, followed by a comma, and then the place name where the event took place.

---

[6] Note that at the present time, TempleReady will not process this date until you complete additional research to identify and calculate the year the event took place using the Gregorian calendar.

Table 18. English Regnal Years

	Beginning of Reign	**End of Reign**
William I the Conqueror	25 Dec 1066	9 Sep 1087
William II Rufus	26 Sep 1087	2 Aug 1100
Henry I	5 Aug 1100	1 Dec 1135
Stephen	26 Dec 1135	25 Oct 1154
Henry II	19 Dec 1154	6 Jul 1189
Richard I	3 Sep 1189	6 Apr 1199
John[7]	27 May 1199	19 May 1216
Henry III	28 Oct 1216	16 Nov 1272
Edward I	20 Nov 1272	7 Jul 1307
Edward II	8 Jul 1307	20 Jan 1327
Edward III	25 Jan 1327	31 Jan 1377
Richard II	22 Jun 1377	29 Sep 1399
Henry IV	30 Sep 1399	20 Mar 1413

[7] John's regnal year began on Ascension Day. His regnal year is calculated each year from Ascension Day following the Roman Catholic religious calendar, not the Julian calendar, as follows:

1	27 May 1199–17 May 1200	7	19 May 1205–10 May 1206	13	12 May 1211–2 May 1212
2	18 May 1200–2 May 1201	8	11 May 1206–30 May 1207	14	3 May 1212–22 May 1213
3	3 May 1201–22 May 1202	9	31 May 1207–14 May 1208	15	23 May 1213–7 May 1214
4	23 May 1202–14 May 1203	10	15 May 1208–6 May 1209	16	8 May 1214–27 May 1215
5	15 May1203 2 Jun 1204	11	7 May 1209–26 May 1210	17	28 May 1215–18 May 1216
6	3 Jun 1204–18 May 1205	12	27 May 1210–11 May 1211	18	19 May 1216–19 May 1216

133

Henry V	21 Mar 1413	31 Aug 1422
Henry VI	1 Sep 1422 13 Oct 1470[8]	4 Mar 1461[9] 11 Apr 1471[10]
Edward IV	4 Mar 1461	9 Apr 1483
Edward V	9 Apr 1483	25 Jun 1483
Richard III	26 Jun 1483	22 Aug 1485
Henry VII	22 Aug 1485	21 Apr 1509
Henry VIII	22 Apr 1509	28 Jan 1547
Edward VI	28 Jan 1547	6 Jul 1553
Jane	6 Jul 1553	19 Jul 1553
Mary	19 Jul 1553[11]	24 Jul 1554
Philip and Mary	25 Jul 1554	17 Nov 1558
Elizabeth I	17 Nov 1558	24 Mar 1603
James I (VI of Scotland)	24 Mar 1603	27 Mar 1625
Charles I	27 Mar 1625	30 Jan 1649[12]
Commonwealth[13]	14 Feb 1649	

[8] Henry was recrowned 13 Oct 1470.

[9] Henry VI was driven off the throne during the War of the Roses in 1461.

[10] Edward IV recaptured Henry VI on 11 Apr 1471.

[11] Mary recorded the beginning of her *second* year of reign as 6 Jul 1554, disregarding Jane's short reign.

[12] Charles I was executed 30 Jan 1649.

[13] During the period known as the Commonwealth, a government by council was installed on 14 Feb 1649. The Kingship was abolished on 17 Mar 1649. The council was dissolved on 20 Apr 1653 and nine days later, on 29 Apr 1653, it was established again. Oliver Cromwell was Lord Protector from 16 Dec 1653 through 3 Sep 1658. Richard Cromwell served as Lord Protector from 3 Sep 1658 through 24 May 1659, when he abdicated the throne.

Charles II	29 May 1660[14]	6 Feb 1685
James II	6 Feb 1685	11 Dec 1688
Interregnum	12 Dec 1688	12 Feb 1689
William III and Mary	13 Feb 1689	27 Dec 1694
William III	28 Dec 1694	8 Mar 1702
Anne	8 Mar 1702	1 Aug 1714
George I	11 Aug 1714	11 Jan 1727
George II	11 Jun 1727	25 Oct 1760
George III	25 Oct 1760	29 Jan 1820

---

[14]The reign of Charles II began at the time of his father's death in 1649, although he did not sit on the throne until 29 May 1660, shortly after he was proclaimed king (on 5 May 1660) during his 12th regnal year.

Significant or Catastrophic Events Used for Dates

Some cultures and sources record events based on significant or catastrophic events rather than using birth or death certificates. For example, you may see something like the following in source documents:

Born 55 years after shipwreck
Died 5 years after the great earthquake

When recording these dates, enter the birth date as "55 years after shipwreck" in the date field, and then enter the location where the event took place in the place name field. Enter the death date as "5 years after the great earthquake" in the date field, and then enter the location where the event took place in the place name field. It is not necessary to attempt to convert these dates into Gregorian calendar dates as most major family history software packages allow entry of these dates.[15]

Example of significant or catastrophic event dating

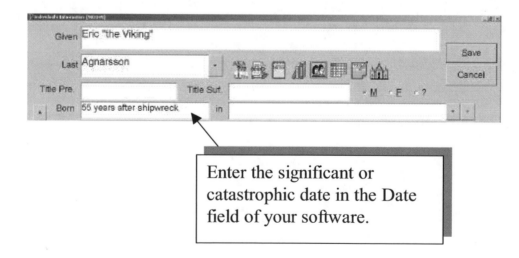

Enter the significant or catastrophic date in the Date field of your software.

---

[15] The current version of TempleReady will not process these dates; however, future versions will. Meanwhile (if you live outside the United States) you can print out immediate family group records within the first four generations and submit them directly to your local temple for processing if you live in a country that uses these dating systems instead of the Gregorian calendar for family history.

Geographic Locations

When you record any date using a family history software program or the paper FGR form, you are trying to record the date on which a specific event occurred at a specific place. Over time, the name of a place may have changed. This can cause great confusion when trying to research your ancestors. Below are four simple rules to make entering places much easier. The differences for entering place information in a software program versus a paper FGR form are described to make sorting and searching your data easier as you continue your research. **Note:** For information on sources that may help you when working with place names, refer to appendix E, Gazetteers and Maps.

Entering Place Names

There are four rules to follow when entering a place name; they are as follows:

Rule One: Always enter the place name as it was called on the day the event took place in the place name field, followed by the current name in the current name field if your software provides this feature.

Example

If your ancestor were born in 1688 in what is now Flatlands, Brooklyn, Kings County, Long Island, New York, USA, the correct entry in your place name field would be:

Amersfoort, Lange Eylandt, Nieuw Nederlandt

The entry in the current name field (if your software provides this feature) would be:

now, Flatlands, Brooklyn, Kings, New York, USA

From this entry you would know what your Dutch ancestors called the place in their documents as well as where to find their records today. By placing a comma between each jurisdiction, each level can be searched in your software and matched with other geographic locale databases. If your software does not provide a current name field, place the current location in the Notes field. You can document a location that changed names several times by entering the following in your Notes field:

later, Flatlands, Long Island, New York

followed by

now, Flatlands, Brooklyn, Kings, New York, USA

Rule Two: Always enter place names beginning with the smallest jurisdiction and ending with the largest.

District, city, town, state, county, province, shire, and country are just a few of the types of civil jurisdictions you will encounter while doing your research. You may use ecclesiastical jurisdictions such as parish, diocese, and country to describe the location of a baptismal, marriage, or other church-related record.

Political descriptions found on some census records will include poll place, ward, precinct, county, state, and country. When describing a rural land record, you may need to use a legal boundary description or section, township, principal meridian, baseline, state, and country to describe a parcel or private cemetery plot. For medieval records, you may use a castle name, followed by a fiefdom and country.

Boundaries on current maps may not correspond with those accepted by Native Americans and other tribal or nomadic peoples. For these populations, use clan, band or totem, tribe or nation, province or state, and country.

When describing a Native American Indian reservation, include it in the order of jurisdictional size from smallest to largest, followed by the state and country. In some cases an allotment number is the smallest place name and is recorded as, for instance, "Allotment 247", in the first place name field.

Exception: You may find exceptions in some cultures where jurisdictions are not necessarily recorded in the order of smallest to largest. Should you encounter this situation, enter the place location in accordance with cultural practices.

Rule Three: List the location at which an event took place with at least three levels of jurisdiction. States and provinces must be followed by their corresponding country name.

The most common way to enter a place name is using city or town as the smallest jurisdiction, followed by the county or parish, then the state, and finally the country. For example:

Stockton, San Joaquin, California, USA

Los Angeles City, Los Angeles County, California, USA

If you are using place names in Connecticut, Maine, Massachusetts, New Hampshire, New Jersey, Pennsylvania, Rhode Island, or Vermont, you may encounter records that use the following more precise way of identifying the place you are recording:

Village, borough or city, town or township, county, state, country

When locale-specific jurisdictional terms such as these are available, you should enter the corresponding place names into your software or paper FGR form in the order indicated here.

If you are using place names in Illinois, Indiana, Kansas, Michigan, Minnesota, North Dakota, Ohio, Oklahoma, South Dakota, Vermont, or Wisconsin, you may encounter records that use the following more precise way of identifying the place you are recording:

City, township, county, state, country

In the states listed in the previous paragraph, some cities will be large enough to not be in a township. In the states of Kansas, Minnesota, North Dakota, Oklahoma, and South Dakota, only unincorporated places are listed with townships.

In Delaware, Louisiana, Maryland, Mississippi, North Carolina, Virginia, and West Virginia, you may encounter the following more precise way of identifying the place you are recording:

Beat, district, precinct, city, county, state, country

Alaska does not have counties as a jurisdictional division. Instead, they use city, borough, senatorial district, state and country.

Again, when you encounter locale-specific jurisdictional terms such as those found in this section, you should enter the corresponding place names into your software or paper FGR form in the order indicated (i.e., smallest to largest jurisdiction). Always include at least three levels of jurisdiction, and include the country name for states and provinces.

Example

Fairbanks, North Star Borough, Central District, Alaska, USA

Independent Cities

There are cities in the United States that are so large that they totally fill the county jurisdiction. When this happens the city and the county can have the same name, as in the instances of Baltimore (in Maryland) and St. Louis (in Missouri). The city of Baltimore is located in the county of Baltimore and the city of St. Louis is located in the county of St. Louis. Records for the city are held independent of the records for the county. To prevent confusion, an independent city is entered with the city name followed by the word "city," then the county name followed by the word "county," then the state and country.

Example

Baltimore City, Baltimore County, Maryland, USA

By doing this, you will save yourself hours of research time when looking for additional research materials.

Military Installations and Territorial Place Names

Military installations are listed followed by the next largest jurisdiction, which may include city, county, state, territory, or country. You may find it helpful to refer to a gazetteer for the appropriate jurisdictions to record a military installation or a territorial place name.

Rule Four: Always spell out the full name of the jurisdiction you are describing (e.g., city, township, county), except for long country names, for example, The United States of America, which is abbreviated USA.

ⓘ Do not use abbreviations for the name of a jurisdiction. You may know exactly what you meant when you abbreviated the name, but the next person you share your data with may not. Abbreviations were first used to enter data on paper FGR forms because they had little room, but most software programs provide ample space to enter the entire name.

Flatlands, Kings, New York, USA

The idea is to be as explicit as possible when describing a location and avoid confusion. The example below is not explicit:

New York

If you entered just "New York" no one else will know if you were referring to the city, the county, or the state of that name.

141

(i) Do not enter a city name without also entering the county information. This will assist you later, when searching (e.g., in a library) for your ancestors from a given area.

(i) Do not use ditto marks (" ") (commonly used to indicate "same information as previous line" on a paper FGR form). Instead, enter the full list of jurisdictions in each individual entry.

When Part or All of a Place Name Is Missing

Some records do not include all the information you need to record a complete place name. When this happens, it is important to indicate what items need further research. If a jurisdictional division is currently unknown, delineate the missing information with commas and a single space, for example:

For a missing city name, use:

, Queens, New York, USA

For a missing county name, use:

Brooklyn, , New York, USA

For missing city and county names, use:

, , New York, USA

Approximating a Place Name

Frequently, prepositions and prepositional phrases are used to further clarify or approximate a location. The prepositional phrase precedes the geographic location being described. Table 19 below provides a list of prepositions and prepositional phrases that are used when describing a location for family history work. Do not abbreviate these phrases when using them as a part of a place name.

142

The most frequently used word is *of.* If the entire place of birth or death is unknown, you may use a place of residence or a place at which you know the individual was living, preceded by the word "of" (lowercase).

Example of using the preposition "of" in a place name

of Flatlands, Kings, New York, USA

ⓘ Do not use question marks or right and left angle brackets (< >). The words "of," "possibly" and "probably" already indicate there is a question to be further researched. Right and left angle brackets indicate your family history software or TempleReady software generated the place name while processing names for ordinance submissions.

Table 19. Prepositions and Prepositional Phrases

Aboard	At the	In	On	Southwest of
Above	Before	In back of	On the	Through
Across	Behind	In front of	Onto	Throughout
Across from	Below	In or near	Out	Toward
Across the	Beneath	Into	Out of	Under
After	Beside	Near	Outside	Underneath
Against	Between	Next to	Outside of	Up
Ahead of	Beyond	North of	Over	West of
Along	By	Northeast of	Past	Within
Along side	Close to	Northwest of	Probably	Without
Among	Down	Of	Possibly	
Around	East of	Off	South of	
At	From	Off of	Southeast of	

Ships as Locations

Many of our ancestors used ships to migrate from one place to another. Each ship left from one port and arrived at another and the ship is considered to be the location of the voyage as well as the location of events that took place on board. Note that your ancestor's place of origin may differ significantly from the port of origin. In some cases, your ancestor may have traveled from one country to another to reach a large port to travel to yet another country. Usually each ship had a name and kept a passenger log. The ship usually sailed between two specific ports. Use the following example style of entry for events, where the ship is the location for a voyage. This will optimize for future research and provide the ability to sort by ship name, port of origin, and port of destination for additional records:

Name of ship, from, name of port, town, parish, province, country, to, name of port, city, county, state, country

For events, such as a birth or death, that took place on board a ship while at sea, ocean, or lake, where the ship name is known, use:

Name of ship, Name of body of water, At Sea

For scattering ashes at sea, refer to Cremation Location on page 147.

At-Sea Locations

All events that occurred at sea but not onboard a ship, such as death by drowning at sea or burial at sea, are recorded by naming the body of water followed by the words "At Sea". If your software provides a field for it, you should also enter the latitude and longitude at the time of the event, as provided on certificates issued after 1837.

Examples of at-sea locations

- **Arctic Ocean, At Sea**
- **Atlantic Ocean, At Sea**
- **Bering Sea, At Sea**

144

- **Hudson Bay, At Sea**
- **Mediterranean Sea, At Sea**
- **Pacific Ocean, At Sea**
- **Sea of Okhotsk, At Sea**
- **Sea of Japan, At Sea**

Lake and River Locations

Some events take place on, near, or in a lake, river, or other named body of water. For these occasions, use the name of the body of water, followed by the name of the jurisdictions, separated by commas, starting from the smallest jurisdiction where the event took place and ending with the largest.

Example of location of events on or in a body of water:

Rio Guadalquivir, Posadas, Andalucia, España

Example of the location of an event that takes place on Lake Washington, near the city of Medina, in Washington State:

Lake Washington, near Medina, King, Washington, USA

Example of the location of an event that takes place where there is no city jurisdiction, on Ames Lake, in a part of rural, unincorporated King County, in Washington State:

Ames Lake, , King, Washington, USA

Example of the location of an event near a body of water but not in or on it. This example takes place near Lake Sammamish, in the city of Bellevue, Washington:

Near Lake Sammamish, Bellevue, King, Washington, USA

145

In-Flight Locations

Occasionally we need to record an event that took place while an individual was in flight, traveling from one destination to another. Occasions may arise in the future for events that take place in space, aboard space stations, and on other celestial bodies.

All events that take place while in flight using private, military, or commercial aircraft between two earthbound locations begin with the words "in flight", followed by the identifying information for the aircraft, followed by the words "while over", followed by the geographic location on earth at the time of the event. The geographic location, whether over land or sea, is always entered beginning with the smallest jurisdiction and ending with the largest, ending with either (1) the country name or (2) the ocean name followed by the words "at sea". This would be used for births, deaths, and marriages while on board an airplane.

Example of the format of an entry for a birth aboard an airplane

In flight, name of airline, flight number, while over, geographic location from smallest to largest, At Sea (or, country name)

All events that take place while in flight using private, military, or commercial aircraft or spacecraft between an earthbound location and a nonearthbound location are entered as follows:

In flight, name of aircraft or spacecraft, flight number, while traveling to (or, from), (then list nonearthbound location, for example, space, space station, planet)

Events that take place on celestial bodies other than the earth are entered using the smallest identifiable geographic location followed by the name of the celestial body or its assigned number.

146

Cremation Location

When an individual has been cremated they are usually not buried in a traditional cemetery burial plot. Ashes can be stored or spread on land, or sea, or over other bodies of water. The following examples will guide you when entering the location of the ashes after cremation.

Examples of cremation locations

For deaths where an individual was cremated and the ashes were scattered over land, use the following style:

> **Cremated, Ashes Spread, Yanno National Park, Flatlands, Kings, New York, USA**

For ashes spread at sea, use:

> **Cremated, Ashes Spread, Pacific Ocean, At Sea**

For ashes stored or buried at a cemetery, use:

> **Cremated, Ashes at Holy Sepulcher Cemetery, Rochester, Monroe County, New York**

For ashes stored at some other location, use:

> **Cremated, Ashes at ... (enter the comma-separated description of the location, starting with the smallest jurisdiction).**

Nonjurisdictional Place Names

Some location descriptions like a street or church should be entered as place names even though they are not themselves jurisdiction names. For example, the name of a street or church may be used as a place name when describing a location. This is common when recording place names in London. The street name or church name being used as a place name is recorded as the smallest jurisdiction (i.e., first) when entering the place name.

(i) Do not include the following nonjurisdictional names in the place name field (the following kinds of place name identification should be included instead in the note or event fields of your software or paper FGR form):

- Address
- Zip code or postal code
- Name of nursing home
- Name of prison or jail
- Name of hospital
- Name of college or university
- Plot number of tombstone

Event Tags

Event tags are used to record information regarding a specific event in your ancestor's life. This section describes a standard set of accepted tags for use in family history. Most family history software comes preprogrammed with these event tags. If your software does not have one or more of these tags, you can create them in the area of your software where you enter events by simply adding new tags.

If your software does not provide a feature to enter information regarding an event tag, or if you are using a paper FGR form, this information may be entered in the Notes field. To enter an event tag in the general Notes field of your software, or in the Notes field of a paper FGR form, follow this sequence of steps:

1. In your Notes field, enter the event tag in all capital letters, followed immediately by a colon (:) then a space.
2. Enter any subevent titles discussed in this section if applicable, followed immediately by the greater-than symbol (>) then a space.
3. Enter the date and place if applicable.
4. Enter any notes regarding the event tag.

Examples of entering main event tag and subevent tags on FGR forms or software that does not provide event tags

Example 1: Main event tag and subevent tag

MARRIAGE: Registration> 13 May 1923 registered to be married in Newark, New Jersey, but was actually married in Princeton, New Jersey a year later.

MARRIAGE: Separation> Oct–Dec 1699, Christabella left her second husband within a few months of the marriage to return to her first husband.

Example 2: Main event tag without a subevent tag

PROPERTY: 1818, purchased the estate of Kidbrook, Susgender, England

149

Accomplishment

This event tag is used to record major successes in your ancestor's life. You may find yourself recording accomplishments that came at great personal expense, or that demonstrate resolve, persistence, or effort ranging from running the Boston Marathon to climbing Mount Everest, from introducing a bill in Congress and having it signed into law, to a great deed of valor on the battle field.

The following are examples of kinds of items that would be recorded using this event tag:

Completion of a goal	Heroic deeds
Fulfillment of a dream	Major successes
Discoveries	Special skills or abilities acquired by training or practice

Achievement

This event tag is only used to record information regarding your ancestor's heraldic insignia. A scanned copy of your ancestor's coat of arms can be attached to this event. The following are typical items to include when using this event tag:

Banners	Coronet	Motto
Cadency	Crest	Seals
Chapeau	Grants of Arms	Shields including dexter and sinister information
Coat of Arms	Helmet	Supporters
Compartment	Mantling	Torse

Adoption

Use this event tag to record any information pertaining to the legal procedure involved in adopting a child. Usually, the adoptive parents are listed as father and mother, and biological parents are listed as the secondary set of parents (both lines are typically traced). Clarification of these relationships is made using this event tag. Issues of privacy should be considered when recording information relating to an adoption. Additionally, information regarding the following subjects is entered using this event tag:

Adoption agency	Biological family	Foster care	Orphans
Adoption services	Changes to birth certificates	Foundlings	Sealed and open adoptions and court records
Attorneys	Foreign agencies	Orphanage	

AKA

Use this event tag if your ancestor used an alias or was otherwise known by a different name or spelling of a name. The alternate name is recorded in the AKA field of the family view of your software. Information regarding legal name changes is also recorded using this event tag. Most software programs come preprogrammed with this event tag in the family view rather than as an event in an event window. If your software does not have this feature in the family view, an event tag called AKA may be used. If you are using a paper FGR form, aliases are recorded in the Notes field. By carefully recording all aliases that your ancestor is known by, you can make full use of your software's search engine and name listings, making it easier to merge files received from or shared with others.

151

Baptism

The basic information relating to an individual's baptism is entered in the family view of your software or the baptism information field of a paper FGR form. Additional information used to clarify your entry for the baptism is recorded in the Notes field that corresponds with the baptismal field in the family view.

If your software does not have this feature or if you are using a paper FGR form, complete the baptism information on your chart, then add your notes to the general Notes field to record additional baptism information. Sources used to record the baptism are noted in the Source field.

Christening specifically refers to a baby who was baptized by sprinkling and given a Christian name; this is one form of baptism and, though entered in the baptismal event field, it should be clarified as a christening in the Notes field. The Notes field should also reflect the method of baptism (e.g., sprinkling or immersion) and list witnesses or godparents who sponsored a child being baptized.

Biography

Use this event tag to record an account of your ancestor's life. Entries in this field will help you portray your ancestors as more than just a collection of names, dates, and places. By including such items as talents, abilities, personal stories, heroic deeds, historical information, manners and customs, journals, hobbies, and travel, to name a few, the ancestor of your records will become a person to be shared with other family members. This is the place for scanned copies of baby books, photograph albums, scrapbooks, letters, diaries, and newspaper clippings. Information regarding family heirlooms and oral traditions are also entered using this event tag.

Birth

The basic information relating to an individual's birth is entered in the family view of your software or the birth information field of a paper FGR form. Additional birth information used to clarify information you are entering is recorded in the Notes field corresponding with the Birth field in the family view of your software.

If your software does not have this birth notes feature, or if you are using a paper FGR form, complete the birth information on your chart and then add your notes to the general Notes field to record additional birth information.

Sources used to record the birth are noted in the Source field.

Birth notes include primary information taken from an affidavit of birth or a birth certificate. Birth certificates include records prepared by, or issued by, municipal jurisdictions, hospitals, physicians, and midwives that officially record the birth of an individual. Note that if a birth occurred at home instead of at an institutional facility, the issuance date of a birth certificate may lag the actual birth by months or years.

Any unusual aspects of a birth certificate should be described in the Notes field for the birth event.

Birth notes are also used to record information extracted from secondary sources such as books and newspapers, or to clarify when a birth date is calculated or approximated based on other data you have regarding your ancestor. For births at sea refer to Ships as Locations on page 144.

On occasion, clarification is required for the birth date, place, or source of information. In modern software programs these can be added to the Notes field for the event in the family view. If your software does not provide this feature, or if using a paper FGR form, use Birth followed by a colon (:) and a single space, then the note in the general Notes field, as illustrated in this example:

Examples of entries for paper FGR form

Birth: Calculated> Aged 29 in 1747 (first marriage date)

Birth: Calculated> Aged 2 years 3 months 8 days on 23 May 1888 (death date)

Birth: Handwriting> birth date may be 12th or 2nd handwriting is difficult to decipher.

Burial

The basic information relating to an individual's burial is entered in the family view of your software or the burial information field of a paper FGR form.

Information obtained from an obituary is recorded as a source, not an event. The full text of an obituary is entered into the source information field or the general Notes field on a paper FGR form.

Unbaptized individuals, excommunicated church members, and those who were buried without religious rites, may be referred to as interred rather than buried. Information regarding interment is recorded in this event field and clarified in the Notes field.

Details regarding the following items are recorded in the Notes field for this event tag:

Bible plate entries for burials	Commercial and Municipal burial grounds	Monumental inscriptions (tombstones, vaults, photographs of gravestones, fallen markers, memorial plaques and statuary)

Body transfers	Cremation; refer also to Cremation on page 147.	Permits
Burials at sea; refer also to page 144.	Funeral cards	Perpetual care
Cemetery address	Genderton's records	Plot registers
Cemetery deeds	Grave openings and postmortem exhumations	Relocated cemeteries
Changes in cemetery names and ownership	Homestead burial grounds	Row and plot number
Church burial grounds and registers		

Census

This event tag is used for all information regarding your ancestor taken from a census. Record the census date and the place where the census was taken using the smallest geographic location to largest (i.e., house number, street, district, ward, city, county, state, and country). The census date is important because the ages recorded on the census date are intended to be correct as of the official census date, even though the census taker had nine months to complete the records. Include the name of the census taker and other details you find in your ancestor's census record. The following are examples of items that may be found using a census record:

Vital Statistics: Name, gender, race, country of origin, names of other household members, relationships, age, head of household status, date of death, place of residence (including house number and street address), adopted or foster children, parents' places of birth, Soundex[16] number
Criminal History: Inmate or convict
Education: Schooling, literacy, ability to speak language of his or her new country, other languages spoken in the home
Financial Information: Agricultural holdings, industrial or manufacturing interests, homelessness, pauper status, employment status, homeowner or renter, mortgage information on real estate, landlord status
Marital Status: Single, married, widowed, divorced
Medical Information: Cause of death; chronic illnesses; diseases; mental deficiencies; impairments of speech, sight, or hearing; physical ailments such as being crippled, maimed or deformed
Military Information: Branch of service, rank, company, veteran status, regiment or ship, war served in, side fought on, dates of enlistment and discharge, duration of service
Naturalization Information: If naturalized, process of naturalization, number of years in country
Occupation: Profession or trade
Servant status: Freeman, indentured servant, slave

---

[16] Researchers group similar-sounding last names together using Soundex codes. This helps to avoid recording errors made by census takers when searching census records.

Condition

This event tag takes the place of many entries that were once recorded in family histories in Latin. The following are some examples that are now recorded in English in this event field:

Examples of uses for the Condition event tag

Latin abbreviation	Latin (do not use)	Use English
d.s.p.	Decessit sine prole	Died without issue
d.s.p.l.	Decessit sine prole legitima	Died without legitimate issue
d.s.p.m.	Decessit sine prole mascula	Died without male issue
d.s.p.m.s.	Decessit sine prole mascula superstite	Died without surviving male issue
d.s.p.s.	Decessit sine prole superstite	Died without surviving issue
d.v.m.	Decessit vita matris	Died in the lifetime of the mother
d.v.p.	Decessit vita partis	Died in the lifetime of the father

A helpful resource for Latin terminology used in genealogical records is: Martin, Charles Trice, compiler *The Record Interpreter: A Collection of Abbreviations, Latin Words and Names Used in English Historical Manuscripts and Records*, second edition, Clearfield Company, Inc: Baltimore 1977, reprint of 1910 edition printed in London.

Court

This event tag is used to record civil and criminal court proceedings and related documents. The following are just a few of the many items that would be recorded using this event tag:

Appeals	Depositions	Minutes	Perjury
Arbitration	Dockets	Name of judge	Statements
Attorney's records	Evidence	Names of the members of a jury	Testimony
Bail Bonds	Grand jury indictments	Names of the parties	Transcripts
Briefs	Injunctions	Notices	Verdicts
Complaints	Interrogatories	Opinions	Warrants
Decisions	Judgments	Petitions	Witnesses
Declarations	Law enforcement records	Pleadings	Writ of summons

Ⓘ Do not use this event tag to record information related to sentencing, incarceration, parole, and penal institutions. Refer to Punishment event tag on page 174.

Ⓘ Do not use this event tag to record information related to litigation for divorce, guardianship, orphans, adoptions, and custodial rights. Refer to Marriage event tag on page 166 and Adoption event tag on page 151.

Crusade

Use this event tag if your ancestor was a crusader. You can indicate the crusade he or she participated in, historical information, campaigns, and additional information in the event tag Notes field. Refer also to the use of Between dating on page 120.

Death

The death date and place are entered in the family view of your software or the death information field of a paper FGR form. This event tag is used to clarify data, other than the actual cause of death, abstracted from death certificates, coroner's reports, law enforcement records and newspaper articles.

Death certificates and obituary citations are entered in the Source field. The full text of an obituary is entered using this event tag.

Ⓘ Do not use the death event tag to enter the cause of death. Cause of death is *always* entered in medical notes or using the Medical event tag. Refer to Medical event tag on page 167.

Education

This event tag is used to record information regarding your ancestor's education. The following are examples of items recorded using this event tag:

Academic interests	Financial aid	Institution addresses	Teachers
Apprentice-ships	Graduation dates	Junior Colleges	Test scores
Awards	Grammar Schools	Junior High Schools	Trade School

159

Boarding Schools	Grants	Middle Schools	Transcripts
Degrees earned	High Schools	Preschools	Tutoring
Diplomas and certificates	Home School	Scholarships	Universities
Fields of specialty	Internships	Teachers	Years Attended

Example of use of Education event tag

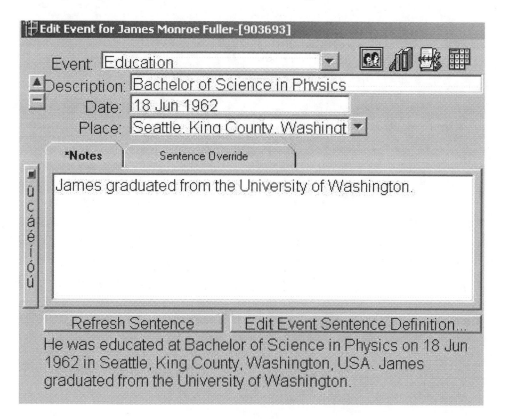

160

Emigration (From)

Use this event tag to record when and where your ancestor left *from* in their native country to live in another country. This event tag is used to record such details as the name of the ship they sailed on, events that occurred during the crossing, and the names of the family members they sailed with. An example of the items you would record using this event tag include:

- Place of ancestor's origin.
- Passports and visas.
- Tickets and travel arrangements.
- Forms of transportation used.
- Name of ship.
- Date and port of departure.
- Passenger departure lists.
- Ship's records, including captain's logs and journals.
- Voyage information.

When recording information about where your ancestor went *to* refer to Immigration (To) event tag on page 164.

ⓘ Do not record information about the naturalization or change in citizenship of your ancestor using this event tag. For information regarding naturalization or citizenship refer to Naturalization event tag on page 170.

ⓘ Do not use the Emigration event tag to record your ancestor moving from one state or province to another, one county to another, or one city or region to another within the same country. These items are recorded using the event tag Residence. Refer to Residence event tag on page 175 for these items.

Example of use of Emigration event tag

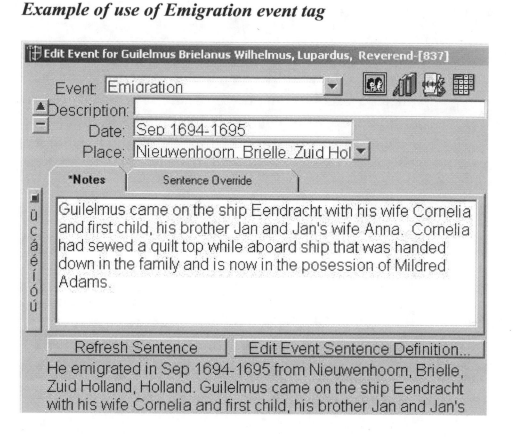

Finances

This event tag is used to record information regarding the finances of your ancestor, for example:

Accounting records	Income tax returns	Real estate taxes
Appurtenances	Investments	Safety deposit boxes
Bankruptcy	Liens	School tax
Business	Personal property	U.S. Securities and Exchange Commission documents (e.g., 10k and 10q)
Corporate taxes	Poll taxes	

162

Example of use of Finances event tag

Add Event to Susan Ann Murphy-[903693]

Event: Finances

Description: Valuation of Estate

Date: 11 Jun 1990

Place: Boulder Creek, Santa Cruz Cou

| *Notes | Sentence Override |

Susan's family lost all of their savings in the stock market crash of 1929. As a result all of her life she was very frugal having lived through the great depression. She accumulated utility and technology stocks in her portfolio until her death in 1990. At the time of her death her estate was valued at $1,873,997.

Refresh Sentence | Edit Event Sentence Definition...

Finances. Valuation of Estate, 11 Jun 1990, Boulder Creek, Santa Cruz County, California, USA. Susan's family lost all of their savings in the stock market crash of 1929. As a result all of

Honors

This event tag is used to record special recognition, awards, or decorations given by others and bestowed upon your ancestor. In all cases, record the date, place, and circumstances of the honor.

The following are examples of items that would be recorded using this event tag:

Awards and badges	Literary awards
Civic and scholastic decorations and medals	Military decorations
Coinage and medallions	Numismatic likenesses
Commemorations	Scientific awards
Endowed chair	Trophies
Honorary doctorates	

Immigration (To)

Use this event tag to record when and where your ancestor entered a new country to live. Items you will record using this event tag include:

- Date and port of entry.
- Passenger arrival lists.
- Border crossing location between two adjacent countries.
- Immigrant aid societies used.
- Denization.
- Reason for immigrating to new country.

When recording information about where your ancestor came *from* refer to Emigration event tag on page 161.

Example of use of Immigration event tag

⊕ Do not record information about the naturalization or change in citizenship of your ancestor using this event tag. For information regarding naturalization or citizenship, refer to Naturalization event tag on page 170.

(i) Do not use the Immigration event tag to record your ancestor moving from one state or province to another, one county to another, or one city or region to another within the same country. These items are recorded using the Residence event tag. Refer to Residence event tag on page 175.

Inquisition

This event tag is used only to record details regarding an inquisition post mortem. Use the Notes field of this event tag to record the full text of writs and reports written in Latin and prepared by escheators for the king.

Kinship

Use this event tag to clarify the relationship of your ancestor to another person.

Examples of Kinship entries for paper FGR form

Kinship: Daughter and Heiress of Walbeck 1325
Kinship: Second son and heir, being first son by second wife
Kinship: Illegitimate son
Kinship: Illegitimate daughter, Legitimated 1427
Kinship: Posthumous son
Kinship: Uterine sister of Sir Ralph Valentine Knight
Kinship: Brother German of Sir Ralph Williamson Baronet

Living

This event tag is used to record that your ancestor was alive as of a certain date and place or period and place. This event tag is usually used when you are missing a death date and have documentation that indicates that your ancestor was alive as of the date of the source document you are using. The term "flourished" is no longer used.

ⓘ Do not use the Living event tag to record a place of residence (refer to Residence event tag on page 175 for that).

Marriage

In most family history software programs, marriage information is entered from the family view and notes are entered into corresponding Notes fields. If you are using software that does not provide this feature, or if you are using a paper FGR form, a Marriage event tag can be added to your general Notes field.

This event tag is used for all information regarding legal and nonlegal marriages, separations, and civil divorces. The following are examples of items that may be recorded using this event tag:

Announcement	Bundling	Engagement
Annulment	Certificate	License
Application	Common Law Marriage	Mistress
Banns (refer also to page 125)	Concubine	Polygamy
Betrothal (also called Espousal)	Consent Notice	Prenuptial Agreement
Bigamy	Contract	Proclamations
Border Marriage	Dispensation	Registration
Charter	Divorce Filing (civil)	Resolemnization
Bonds	Divorce Finalized (civil)	Separation
Bridal Registry	Dowry	Settlement

(i) Do not record religious proceedings to obtain a divorce recognized by a specific religious denomination using this event tag. For a Jewish divorce (a "Get") and a LDS cancellation of sealing use the religion event tag. Refer to Religion event tag on page 175.

Medical

Most family history software now provides an area designated for medical notes. The Medical event tag is used if your software does not provide this feature or if you are using a paper FGR form. The following are examples of items that may be recorded using this event tag:

Allergies	Hospitalizations	Medical records
Autopsy	Immunizations	Mental health records
Coroner's reports such as necropsy and pathology reports	Injuries	Operations, procedures or surgeries
Cause of death, including murder, manslaughter, unnatural, or unknown causes	Insurance records	Prescriptions
Dental records	Major illness	X-rays
Diseases	Medical examiner's notes and reports	
Genetic disorders	Medical histories	

167

Examples of Medical entries for paper FGR forms

Medical: Cause of Death> 1899, Charles died of influenza in his daughter's home at 503 Humboldt Lane.

Medical: Injury> Fred lost right leg in Vietnam stepping on a land mine.

Medical: Genetic Disorder> Susan was carrier of recessive gene for Congenital Sucrase Isomaltase Deficiency on the third chromosome.

Membership

All organizations that your ancestor was a member of are recorded under this event tag. Charitable, fraternal or sororal, genealogical, historical, and social are just some of the many organizations your ancestor may have participated in. Include the duration of membership, place, duties and responsibilities, and functions sponsored or attended.

Examples of paper FGR form entry

Membership: 1988-2001, Daughters of the American Revolution

Membership: 11 Jan 1988 to 2000, New England Historical and Genealogical Society

Military

This event tag is used to record all information—other than awards, honors, or decorations—regarding your ancestor's military service record. The following are examples of items that may be recorded using this event tag:

Battle rolls	Payment registers
Campaigns	Pension records
Discharge	Prisoner of war records
Enlistment	Rank
Militias	Regiment
Missions	Special assignments
Muster rolls	Veteran's benefits
Orders	War served in

If your ancestor was not in the military but lived through a war, refer to War event tag on page 180.

For information on how to enter military titles before given names and after surnames, refer to Titles event tag on page 179 and see also the Military event tag on page 168.

🛈 Do not record military awards, honors, or decorations using this event tag. Refer to Honors event tag on page 163.

Mission

Use to this event tag for all religious denominations to record where a missionary served, the nature of the work performed, the dates of service and other notes that may describe the mission.

Namesake

Use this event tag to describe the details of who your ancestor is named after, research on persons with the same surname, and one-name family history societies.

Nationality

Use this event tag to record your ancestor's nationality if different than that of the country your ancestor lived in or died in. This includes the status of belonging to a nation by birth, naturalization, or origin (before state records were kept).

Naturalization

This event tag is used for all information regarding naturalization and citizenship. The following are examples of items that may be recorded using this event tag:

- Affidavits.
- Alien registration.
- Citizenship papers.
- Declarations of Intention.
- Green cards.
- Initial voter registration records.
- Oaths of allegiance.
- Petitions.
- Work permits.
- Deportation.

Occupation

This event tag is used to record apprenticeships, employment information, personnel records, promotions, profession, trade, and avocation. Include dates of service or employment, and place when applicable. Information gleaned from telephone directories, business cards, and advertisements that your ancestor may have published are

170

also entered using this tag. To record indentured apprenticeships refer to Slavery event tag on page 176.

Office

Use this event tag to record elected partisan, nonpartisan, or appointed public office held in all municipal jurisdictions, including school boards, water commissions, precinct committees, wards, or other public boards or commissions.

Physical

Use this event tag to describe physical attributes such as eye color, hair color, physical stature, and facial features of your ancestor.

Politics

Use this event tag to record what political ideology or political party your ancestor was associated or registered with (i.e., communist, socialist, democrat, greens, republican, libertarian, and so on). It can be used to record where they fall on the political spectrum (liberal, moderate, conservative), political volunteerism, causes participated in, public policy created, and lobbying activities. Some individuals are involved in politics only for a single issue or a narrow number of related issues; these are also recorded using this event tag.

If your ancestor held or was appointed to a public office, refer to Office event tag, above. This event tag can be used if an individual ran for public office but was not elected in a partisan or nonpartisan race.

Probate

This event tag is used for all information regarding probate, except wills, which are listed separately. The following are examples of items that may be recorded using this event tag:

Appeals	Judgments
Codicils	Living will
Conservator-ship	Letters of Administration
Debtors	List of heirs
Dower	Power of Attorney
Estates	Testament
Executors	Trusts
Guardianship	Witnesses
Inventory	

(i) Do not use this event tag to record information or the content of a will. Refer to Will event tag on page 180.

Property

This event tag is used for all information regarding property controlled, acquired, sold, or lost by your ancestor. The following are examples of items that may be recorded using this event tag:

Assessments	Grants	Plat books
Atlases	Head rights	Preservation societies
Bill of sale	Histories of old houses	Purchases
Certificate	Historical land and building designations	Real estate transaction records
Claims	Homesteads	Rental agreements
Contracts	Indentures	Quit Claim
Deeds	Leans	Street Maps
Easements	Leases	Structures built
Entry case files	Mortgages	Survey
Equity notices	Options	Tenants
Foreclosure	Parcel Maps	Trust
Founded (an abbey, etc.)	Parcel Numbers	Warrant
Gazetteers	Patents	

Punishment

This event tag is used for all information regarding punishments and related items sustained by your ancestor. The following are examples of items that may be recorded using this event tag:

Attainders	Paroles
Banishments	Penal institutions (including names and locations of jails and prisons)
Names of dungeons or castle towers	Probations
Executions	Required duties in public service
Fines and penalties	Seizures of real and personal property
Incarcerations	Stays
Pardons	Whippings

Religion

This event tag is used to record all information that pertains to the spirituality, religious context, or religious experiences of your ancestor, including religious customs, practices, and special ordinances that your ancestor may have received or participated in during his or her lifetime. The following items will give you an idea of just some of the items you would record using this event tag:

Blessings	Holy Communion	Religious movements
Confirmations	Miracles	Religious persecutions
Names and dates of congregations attended	Last rights	Unctions
Conversions from one faith to another	Letters of introduction	Removals
Denominations	Ministers' records and journals	Subscription lists
Disciplinary actions, including disfellowship, and excommunication	Patron saints and martyrs	Trials of faith

Residence

This event tag is used to record information documenting that your ancestor was living in a certain place at a certain time. This event tag is also used to record incidences of your ancestor migrating or moving from and to one of the following:

175

- Region to region.
- State to state.
- County to county.
- City to city.
- Pioneer migrations.
- Territorial migrations.
- Forced migrations, including evictions (e.g., disseisin).

⬤ Do not use this event tag to record your ancestor moving from one country to another. Refer to Emigration (From) event tag on page 161 and Immigration (To) event tag on page 164.

Retirement

This event tag is used to record the date of retirement, age of retirement, the firm retired from, pension application, pension benefits, place of retirement, and activities during retirement. It is also used to record whether the person retired early and the circumstances surrounding voluntary or forced retirement.

Slavery

This event tag is used to record information regarding all forms of servitude. Record available details pertaining to indentured servitude (including contracted servitude prior to a voyage), indentured apprenticeships, redemptioners (selling oneself into servitude upon arrival for a period of time to pay for passage), and slavery (all forms). Items usually included using this event tag are information about:

- Contracts.
- Bills of sale.
- Plantation records.
- Underground railroad.
- Runaway slaves.
- Terms of servitude.
- Dates of servitude.
- Freedman's savings and trust accounts.

- The Bureau of Refugees.
- Manumission certificates.

For help entering the given name and surname of a slave, refer to page 48.

Social Security Number

Use this event tag to record information from an Application for a Social Security Number (SSN), the issued social security number, Social Security Benefit Application for Disability, Social Security Retirement Benefits, or a Social Security Notification of Death.

Sports

This event tag is used to record the sports and athletic activities of your ancestor. This can include such items as memberships in team sports such as children's leagues, high school and college teams, professional teams, company tournaments, games and competitions, national and Olympic events; athletic abilities; athletic achievements; sports-related awards and scholarships; statistics; and team lore.

Surname

This event tag is used to clarify changes in your ancestor's surname. It is specifically used in the following cases:

- When a surname not previously hyphenated becomes hyphenated.
- When a surname changes because a new feudal estate is acquired.
- When the surname of the child differs from the surname of the male parent.
- When the surname of the mother is used instead of the father.
- When the surname is changed because of adoption or other court proceedings regarding custody or guardianship of a child.
- When an individual legally changes his or her surname.
- When an individual assumes an alias surname.
- When multiple documents record various spellings of your ancestor's surname.
- When a portion of the surname is dropped or truncated.
- When, upon immigration or naturalization, the surname is partially or totally changed.
- When the surname has been anglicized or translated into a language not spoken by your ancestor.

Titles

This event tag is used to indicate when an individual obtained a peerage title and to clarify details about when a title was created or used. This tag is also used to clarify times when the husband held a peerage title but the wife did not, and cases where a title was styled or otherwise inappropriately used.

Example

Edit Event for Sylvester Van Noordwickie-[12726]

Event: Title

Description: 3rd count of Noordwijke

Date: 16 Jan 1327-1328

Place: Noordwijk, Zuid Holland, Hollar

*Notes | Sentence Override

Became the third count of Noordwijke after killing his uncle in battle. His wife did not become the countess of Noordwijke as she died in 1314 prior to Sylvester becoming a count.

Refresh Sentence | Edit Event Sentence Definition...

Title. 3rd count of Noordwijke, 16 Jan 1327-1328, Noordwijk, Zuid Holland, Holland. Became the third count of Noordwijke after killing his uncle in battle. His wife did not become the countess of Noordwijke as she died in 1314 prior to Sylvester

179

War

Use this event tag to record the name and details of a war that your ancestor lived through or died in. If your ancestor participated in military service see Military event tag on page 168.

For additional reference material on wars and other military engagements see:

Brassey's Dictionary of Battles by John Laffin, Barnes and Noble Books: New York, 1995.

The Oxford Companion to American Military History edited by John Whiteclay Chambers II; Oxford University Press: New York, 1999.

Will

Use this event tag to record the date, place, and entire text of your ancestor's will. Wills may be written several years or days or even merely hours prior to the demise of your ancestor. Your notes should reflect the date the will was signed or recorded, and include the names of the witnesses and executors. Indicate whether you are recording the full text of the will, or an extract or abstract of the will. If multiple wills were made during the life of your ancestor, reference them in date order, and include their full text. Refer also to Probate on page 172.

E. Research Tags

Whenever further research on an item is required, enter the type of research needed and then enter all related citations. By using standardized research tags discussed in this section, you can use the search features in your family history software to create lists or reports of items that require further attention.

Items requiring more in-depth research may be entered into your research notes if your software offers this feature, or may be entered in the Notes field for a specific Research tag if it does not.

Abeyance

This research tag is used only to record information about a peerage whose inheritance has become unclear. This usually happens when more than one heir is equally entitled to inherit a barony created by a writ of summons. The abeyance will continue until all but one female line of descent with the right of inheritance becomes extinct.

This research tag is *not* used to record a dormant or extinct peerage, cases where no potential heir can be traced, or cases where a holder died leaving no heir. To enter dormant or extinct peerage, use the Title event tag. Refer to Title event tag on page 179.

Alt Baptism

Use this research tag when you have more than one reliable source but the sources give conflicting information regarding the baptism of your ancestor. This type of entry might include any one or combination of the following:

- Baptismal date.
- Congregation.
- Denomination.
- Place.

Alt Birth

Use this research tag when you have more than one reliable source but the sources give conflicting information regarding the birth of your ancestor. This type of entry might include any one or combination of the following:

- The date of birth.
- Place of birth.
- Circumstances regarding the birth.
- Explanations of possible alternate parents.
- Birth order.

Alt Burial

Use this research tag when you have more than one reliable source but the sources give conflicting information regarding the burial of your ancestor. This type of entry might include any one or combination of the following:

- Date of burial.
- Type of burial or cremation.
- Locale of burial.
- Name of cemetery.
- Incorrect plot number.

Alt Death

Use this research tag when you have more than one reliable source but the sources give conflicting information regarding the death of your ancestor. This type of entry might include any one or combination of the following:

- Date of death.
- Place of death.
- Circumstances surrounding the death of your ancestor.

Assumption

This research tag is used when you are entering data that is believed to be true for which you have no proof or documentation or for which you are relying on meager and inconclusive materials.

Example of use of Assumption research tag

Challenged

This research tag is used when you wish to record family history information that has come into question. This tag is most frequently used when new information is brought to light that brings long established succession in a family line into question.

Conclusion

This research tag is used when you are entering data that is based on a decision or an opinion you have formed based on the logical use of

183

solid documentation. This data is based on facts or evidence accumulated while researching your ancestor but for which you are lacking definitive proof.

Conflict

Occasionally, sources will disagree about a specific item pertaining to your ancestor. When this happens, use this research tag. This research tag can include problems with dates, given names, surnames, place names, events, and parents or lineages.

Example of use of Conflict research tag

184

Disproven

This research tag is used to document a lineage that has been conclusively disproven. This research tag is also used to record the evidence used to disprove the lineage.

Error

Occasionally errors are found when compiling information about your ancestor. Use this research tag to document these errors. Some of the types of errors you may find are:

- Typographical errors.
- Information for one event that was accidentally recorded or entered for another event.
- Documents that were misinterpreted or misread.
- Information given during personal interviews that is found to be incorrect when substantiated by vital records.
- Records of siblings or parents that are incorrectly associated with your ancestor's family.

Example of the use of the Error research tag

Add Event to Sylvester Van Noordwickie

Event: Error

Description: Typographical error

Date: 9 Aug 2001

Place:

*Notes | Sentence Override

In History of the Van Noordwijck Family by Sally Van Noordwijck, Dutch Publishing Company, Seattle, Washington, 1999 page 209 indicated the birth date as 13 July 1888, page 388 of the same book contains a typographical error listing the christening date as 27 August 1888 as the birthdate.

Refresh Sentence | Edit Event Sentence Definition...

Error. Typographical error, 9 Aug 2001. In History of the Van Noordwijck Family by Sally Van Noordwijck, Dutch Publishing Company, Seattle, Washington, 1999 page 209 indicated the birth date as 13 July 1888, page 388 of the same book

185

Investigate

If your software does not provide an area to record research notes or if you are using a paper FGR form, you can use this research tag to record items requiring further research. These items are recorded by using a one-word summary for the type of research to be done, followed by a colon (:) and space, then by a description of the research to be completed.

Example of the use of the Investigate event tag

F. Ordinance Information

The information contained in this section is provided for the use of members of The Church of Jesus Christ of Latter-day Saints in preparing record submissions in order that the gospel ordinances of salvation can be performed by the living on behalf of their ancestors, in temples consecrated for that purpose, and to record the completed temple work.

All baptized members of the Church of Jesus Christ may make submissions for proxy temple ordinances. There are four ordinances that can be included in a temple ordinance submission. They are: baptism (B), endowment (E), sealing of parents to children—known as sealing to parents (SP), and sealing of parents to each other—known as sealing to spouse (SS). The goal of all temple ordinances, including these proxy ordinances facilitated by family history research, is to enable family members, living or dead, to be united together for time and eternity as an eternal family, regardless of whether the sacred ordinances were received by your ancestors during their mortal life.

Terminology

GEDCOM Files

A GEDCOM (or Genealogical Data Communications) file is an internationally accepted computer file format initially created by the Family History Department of the Church of Jesus Christ of Latter-day Saints, and is now accepted worldwide as a common format for sharing family history files. GEDCOM files are used for transferring and receiving genealogical information and associated notes and source information between computers, between software programs, and over the Internet. All family history software produced by the Church of Jesus Christ of Latter-day Saints, including products and Internet sites, uses this format. This includes FamilySearch™, TempleReady, and PAF. All of the major commercially available family history software products and Internet databases also import and export files in this format. You must use a GEDCOM file to submit information to TempleReady, Ancestral File, Pedigree Resource File™, and other online Internet family history databases such as GENDEX and Ancestry.com.

187

You currently cannot use GEDCOM files to transfer scanned images linked to your individual records because support for this capability is nearly nonexistent among various genealogy software programs. Scanned pictures and documents should be transferred separately.

FamilySearch

FamilySearch is a group of databases compiled by the Church of Jesus Christ of Latter-day Saints to assist you with your family history. FamilySearch can be found on the Internet at http://www.familysearch.org/, in Salt Lake City at the Family History Library, or at one of the branch Family History Resource Centers located worldwide in local Church of Jesus Christ of Latter-day Saints branch, ward, and stake buildings and facilities.

FamilySearch currently consists of the following databases and software:

- Pedigree Resource File.
- International Genealogical Index.
- Ancestral File.
- Social Security Death Index.
- Military Index.
- Family History Library Catalog.
- Vital records (currently only portions of these are available on the Internet).
- TempleReady (currently not available on the Internet).

International Genealogical Index

The International Genealogical Index, or IGI as it is more commonly known, consists of more than 285 million individual records compiled from sources worldwide. All but a few million of these names were extracted from original government and church vital records from 1500 to the early 1900s. Some branch Family History Centers hold this collection for patron use on CD-ROM. Each record includes one of the following:

- Name of individual, birth date and place, name of parents if included in the original vital record.

- Name of individual, christening date and place, name of parents if included in the original vital record.

- Name of individual, marriage date and place, and name of spouse.

Ancestral File and Ancestral File Numbers

The Ancestral File is a family history information database created by the Church of Jesus Christ of Latter-day Saints containing the records of nearly 35 million individuals in linked family files. This database consists of individual and family records, including about 1.5 million individuals of royal lines representing the major regions of the world, most of the genealogies of famous people, prominent LDS pioneer lines, and prominent Yankee, colonial, and revolutionary records. Compilation of this database began in 1979 based on international LDS member submissions and extraction programs. Much of this database does not contain adequate source notes, so the information must be verified before you can rely on it.

Each individual in the Ancestral File has been assigned a unique Ancestral File Number, or AFN for short. The AFNs usually consist of four numbers and/or letters, then a hyphen followed by two additional numbers and/or letters. The largest AFN cannot exceed 20 characters, including hyphens.

189

Example of an AFN entry

The following illustration for Richard Tempest shows an entry
for the AFN: X9LB-F2.

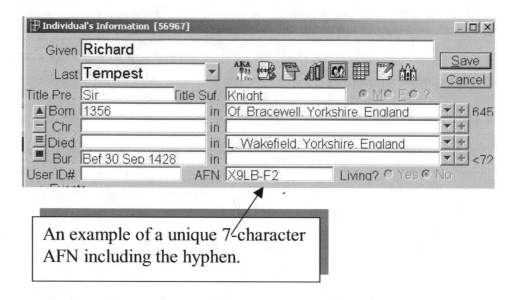

An example of a unique 7-character
AFN including the hyphen.

Pedigree Resource File

The Pedigree Resource File is a genealogical information
database created by the Church of Jesus Christ of Latter-day
Saints containing the records of nearly 40 million individuals in
linked family files. The database includes individual records,
records of parents, and researcher information. Some records
include sources and other notes, also AFN numbers if provided
by the submitters. Submitters may be contacted through e-mail
for sources and additional notes. Submissions to this file may be
made in either of two ways: (1) by using the FamilySearch
Internet Genealogy Service to submit GEDCOM files (see
http://www.familysearch.org/ENG/default.asp), and (2), through
a systematic effort to gather and input government archives.
Close to 1.5 million names are submitted each month by
researchers like yourself who want to share and collaborate with
others working on the same family lines.

Creating Temple Ordinance Submissions

The following guidelines apply when submitting the records of an ancestor for temple ordinances:

1. **Children who died before the age of eight are not submitted for baptism or endowment**.

   Children who died before the age of 8 are not considered to be accountable or in need of receiving individual ordinances and hence would be submitted for sealing only to the parents. If a child died before the age of 3, the word "Infant" is entered in the date field for both the baptism and endowment ordinances. This is true for both software and paper FGR form entries. If the child died between the ages of 3 and 8, the word "Child" is entered in the date field for both the baptism and endowment ordinances.

   Example of entering a child who died before the age of eight for sealing to parents

By entering the word Infant or Child in the date fields, you correctly prevent your software from inappropriately creating a submission record for Baptism or Endowment work. This child would be submitted only for sealing to the parents.

LDS Ordinance Information

Husband: Philipus Van Noordwijck-[1
Date

Baptism | Child
Endowment | Child
Seal to Par / BIC
Parents...

Wife:
Date
Baptism
Temple
Endowment
Seal to Par / BIC
Parents...

Marriage Ordinance
Date | Temple
Sealed to Spouse

Repeat | Save | Cancel | Help

2. **Children who are stillborn are not submitted for temple ordinances**.

If a child was born stillborn, enter "Stillborn" in the date field for all four ordinances. This is true for both software and paper FGR form entries.

Example of an entry for a stillborn child

Temple submissions are not made for children who are listed as stillborn except in the countries listed below. The word stillborn is entered in each of the four date fields, correctly preventing a temple submission from being made.

In the countries listed below, it was the custom to record children who lived only a short time as stillborn, thus it is permissible to submit these children for sealing to parents. In this case the word "Infant" is entered into the birth and endowment date fields, and the sealing to parents field is left blank. Your software will then generate the correct submission for this child to be sealed to his or her parents.

Table 20. Countries That List Children Who Lived for a Short Period of Time as Stillborn

Austria	Italy
Belgium	Liechtenstein
Czechoslovakia	Luxemburg
Denmark	Netherlands
Finland	Norway
France	Poland
Germany	Sweden
Hungary	Switzerland
Iceland	

3. **Children who are born in the covenant are not submitted for sealing to parents**.

If a child was born in the covenant (i.e., the parents were already sealed together at the time of the child's birth), enter "BIC" in the sealed to parents date field. All other temple ordinances may be submitted.

Example of entering a child born in the covenant

Enter BIC in the date field for sealing to parents for children born in the covenant.

4. **If your deceased ancestor was born within 95 years of the present date, you cannot submit this individual for temple ordinances unless your ancestor's** *closest living relative* **has given permission. You may submit records of your deceased ancestor for temple ordinances one year after their death if permission has been received.**

The closest living relative has priority in submitting this ancestor for temple ordinances. If you are not the closest living relative and permission cannot be obtained from the closest living relative, the temple ordinance submission must be postponed until permission is received. You will not be acting in accordance with church policy if you act contrary to the wishes of the closest living relative.

It is also a church policy to wait one year from your ancestor's death date before submitting their name for temple ordinance work.

If there is a reason not to submit an individual for temple ordinances now, enter the words "do not submit" in the date field for each of the four ordinances. Next, indicate the circumstances in the Notes field.

Example of preventing an individual from being submitted for all temple ordinances

5. **You must have a date and a place for a birth, christening, or death in order to submit an individual's records for temple ordinances.**

   It is the submitter's responsibility to provide adequate identifying information for each ancestor for whom you desire temple ordinance work to be performed. Your information needs to be documented and sources identified prior to your submission. Dates and places may be approximated, but all care should be taken to submit the most accurate record possible when making a submission.

6. **Place names should not be abbreviated, and should be as complete as possible**.

   There must be a minimum of three jurisdictions, from smallest to largest, recorded in the place name field for the birth, christening, or death date. Every place name must end with a state or province and a country name. It is important to enter place name data in as complete a form as possible without abbreviations.

7. **All previously completed temple ordinances must be entered into your software or paper FGR form prior to creating a temple ordinance submission**.

   Except when submitting the names of immediate family members (refer to item 11 below), all entries of ancestors who are being submitted for temple ordinance submissions must be checked to avoid duplication of ordinances. Each ancestor's name must be checked against the International Genealogical Index (IGI) and the Ancestral File for completed ordinance work prior to submitting an individual name in TempleReady. These two databases contain different data obtained from different input sources. Only after completing this research can temple ordinance submissions be created for uncompleted ordinances.

Your ancestor's name may be in these databases under a slightly different spelling, or with approximated dates. A name like Matilda De Clair may need to be searched for under Matilda of Clair, Matilda Clair, Maude De Clair, Maud De Clair, Matilda Declair and Maud Clair as well. It is important to prevent duplications in temple submissions.

8. **Names of individuals born prior to 200 A.D. are not submitted for temple ordinances.**

   It is the current church policy not to process names for temple ordinances for persons born prior to 200 A.D.

9. **The Medieval Family Unit, rather than TempleReady, clears Temple ordinance submissions containing the names of individuals born between 200 A.D. and 1500 A.D.**

   To avoid duplication of temple ordinances, the Medieval Family Unit clears individuals born between 200 and 1500 A.D. Each submission made to the Medieval Family Unit must first be checked in both the International Genealogical Index (IGI) and Ancestral File for completed ordinances before that submission may be made to the unit. Alternate spellings of the names of your ancestors selected for submission must also be checked.

   After carefully checking your ancestors for completed temple ordinances, temple submissions for processing in TempleReady may be made. It is advisable to make submissions in groups of 100 names or less per file. TempleReady files prepared by your family history software are sent to the address below, instead of taking them to your local church family history resource center or the Family History Library, for you to process through the TempleReady software.

If you are using paper FGR forms, you may make TempleReady files for submission by entering your data into family history software provided at local church family history libraries.

Mail submissions to:

Family History Department
Attention: Medieval Family Unit
50 East North Temple Street
Salt Lake City, Utah 84150-3400

10. **Temple ordinance submissions containing the records of individuals born after 1500 A.D. are cleared using TempleReady prior to sending the submission disk to a local temple.**

Most family history software programs have features to create temple ordinance submissions. Several programs pre-qualify your ancestor's information, creating submissions that include only those ancestors for whom you have enough information to qualify for ordinance work and reducing the time required to clear names using TempleReady. These submissions are done automatically after you indicate which of your ancestors' names you wish to submit. If you do not know how to access TempleReady, or you are making a temple ordinance submission using a paper FGR form, contact your ward or stake Family History Consultant for assistance. Your Family History Consultant will have complete instructions on the use of TempleReady and submission of paper FGR forms for your local temple. If you do not have access to TempleReady, you may send your temple ordinance submission file or paper FGR form to:

In the United States and Canada:

> Family History Department
> Attention: Names Submission
> 50 East North Temple Street
> Salt Lake City, Utah 84150

International:

> Send your information to your nearest temple.

11. **A paper FGR form is used when you are submitting immediate family members for temple ordinance submissions.**

A paper FGR form should be used when submitting father, mother, siblings, or children for temple ordinances. This form may be printed from your software, or be typewritten or carefully hand-printed using black ink on a paper FGR form. It is not necessary for immediate family members' names to be cleared through TempleReady prior to their submission to the temple of your choice. The paper FGR form is taken directly to your local temple on the day of your appointment.

12. **TempleReady Submissions may be mailed to the temple of your choice.**

Once you have completed processing your ancestors using TempleReady, the resulting submission may be mailed to the temple of your choice. Mailing addresses may be found in your local church Family History Resource Center or Family History Library.

13. **Make appointments with the temple of your choice to complete your ancestor's temple work.**

If you have elected to complete all temple ordinances yourself, after clearing your ancestors' names using the TempleReady software at your local Family History Resource Center or Family History Library, you must schedule appointments with the temple of your choice to complete the work. This includes scheduling temple sessions to participate in proxy baptisms, marriages, and sealings for your ancestors. Endowments do not require appointments but do require that the previous ordinances have been completed. The temple staff will inform you of all arrangements you will need to make prior to your temple session.

Once you have elected to do the temple ordinances yourself, you are responsible for seeing that all of the ordinances are completed.

You may need the help of others to complete some ordinances. You may solicit the help of ward members by contacting your High Priest Group Leader, family members, or personal friends. All arrangements for assistance should be made prior to your coming to the scheduled temple sessions.

14. **When your ward or stake Family History Consultant cannot provide you with the answer to your questions for special situations, you may contact the Temple Department**.

For all questions regarding ordinance standards and special situations, contact:

Temple Department
50 East North Temple
Salt Lake City, Utah, 84150

Queries to the Temple Department might address, for example, situations regarding ordinance work for a friend, adoption, annulment, divorce, illegitimate children, common-law marriage, special custody or guardianship issues, cases where an individual was raised by someone other than a parent, etc.

Recording Completed Temple Ordinances

If you completed the temple ordinances for your ancestors yourself, you can enter the ordinance information directly into your software or paper FGR form. If you elected to have the temple arrange for others to complete your ancestor's ordinances, you will be able to obtain the completed ordinance information from the next update of the IGI. Enter the date the ordinance was completed and the temple code in the corresponding fields of your family history software or paper FGR form. For a list of temple codes, refer to appendix B, LDS Temple Codes by City, on page 222.

If the date and temple are unknown, but you are sure the ordinances were performed, enter "Done" in the ordinance date field.

II. Pedigree Charts

Pedigree charts are summary charts of information previously recorded in the family view of your software, or on paper versions of an FGR form. Pedigree charts visually link one generation to the next, and can be used to depict both your ancestor's ascendancy (ancestors or progenitors) or descendancy (descendants) lines. By using a pedigree chart, you have very quick access to direct line (i.e., fraternal and maternal blood lines) family relationships. Many genealogists limit the use of the term "family tree" to mean a male line descent from a common ancestor. This is frequently used to determine authorized usage of heraldic insignias. This type of descendancy is also known as a tabular chart. Pedigree charts may be preprinted paper forms that you fill in by hand, or software-generated forms.

There are four widely used preprinted blank paper versions of a pedigree chart that are commercially available, and several software-generated versions that can also be printed as blank forms or can be printed with all the information already filled in from your family history software, including pictures if desired.

Four-Generation Pedigree Chart

The first kind of preprinted pedigree chart is a four-generation pedigree chart. It begins with a single individual and includes his or her spouse, parents, grandparents, and great-grand parents. A completed sheet will list eight families. The lines are laid out from left to right with the youngest generation on the left and the oldest on the right. Many four-generation European charts run from top to bottom, in which the oldest generation is on the top and the youngest is on the bottom.

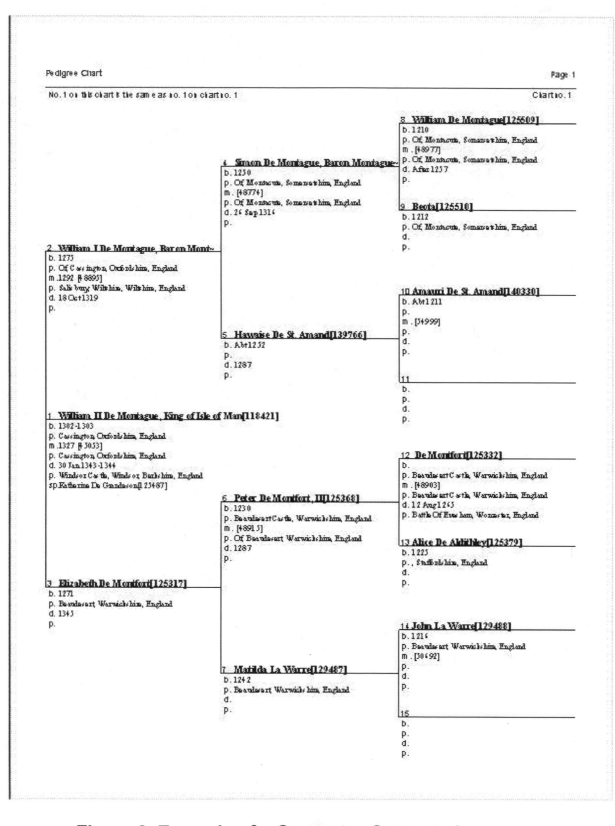

Figure 2. Example of a Computer-Generated
Four-Generation Pedigree Chart

Multiple-Generation Pedigree and Ancestry Charts

The second kind of preprinted blank pedigree chart is a multiple-generation pedigree chart ranging from five to fifteen generations. This is a great research tool because on one piece of paper you will have every line you are working on. It is easy to carry into a library, whereas a computer or tomes of books and binders are not. It is easy to add multiple-generation charts for lines you are successful with. Computer-generated forms can be made from 1 to 250 generations depending on the size of your database. Please refer to Figures 3a and 3b, as examples of Computer-Generated Eight-Generation Ancestry Charts.

Fan Chart

The third kind of preprinted pedigree chart is a fan chart. It can look like a fan or a double fan or circle. Fans place the father's ancestry on the left and the mother's on the right. Double fans or circle charts place the father's ancestry on the top and the mother's on the bottom. These are usually very large wall charts that can be purchased as preprinted blank charts, or family history software can generate them to include the individuals in your database. Please refer to Figure 4 as an example of a computer-generated double fan chart and Figure 5 as an example of a computer-generated single fan chart.

Ancestry Chart of George Henry Fuller

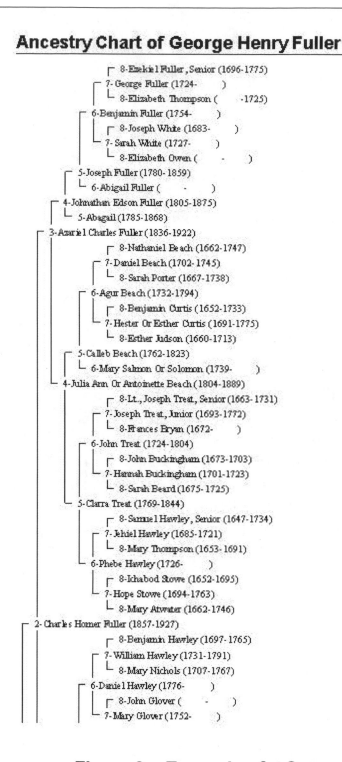

┌ 8-Ezekiel Fuller, Senior (1696-1775)
┌ 7- George Fuller (1724-   )
│ └ 8-Elizabeth Thompson (-1725)
┌ 6-Benjamin Fuller (1754-   )
│ ┌ 8-Joseph White (1683-   )
│ └ 7- Sarah White (1727-   )
│   └ 8-Elizabeth Owen (-   )
┌ 5-Joseph Fuller (1780-1859)
│ └ 6-Abigail Fuller (-   )
┌ 4-Johnathan Edson Fuller (1805-1875)
│ └ 5-Abagail (1785-1868)
┌ 3-Azariel Charles Fuller (1836-1922)
│   ┌ 8-Nathaniel Beach (1662-1747)
│   ┌ 7-Daniel Beach (1702-1745)
│   │ └ 8-Sarah Porter (1667-1738)
│   ┌ 6-Agur Beach (1732-1794)
│   │ ┌ 8-Benjamin Curtis (1652-1733)
│   │ └ 7-Hester Or Esther Curtis (1691-1775)
│   │   └ 8-Esther Judson (1660-1713)
│   ┌ 5-Caleb Beach (1762-1823)
│   │ └ 6-Mary Salmon Or Solomon (1739-   )
│   └ 4-Julia Ann Or Antoinette Beach (1804-1889)
│   ┌ 8-Lt., Joseph Treat, Senior (1663-1731)
│   ┌ 7-Joseph Treat, Junior (1693-1772)
│   │ └ 8-Frances Bryan (1672-   )
│   ┌ 6-John Treat (1724-1804)
│   │ ┌ 8-John Buckingham (1673-1703)
│   │ └ 7-Hannah Buckingham (1701-1723)
│   │   └ 8-Sarah Beard (1675-1725)
│   └ 5-Clarra Treat (1769-1844)
│   ┌ 8-Samuel Hawley, Senior (1647-1734)
│   ┌ 7-Jehiel Hawley (1685-1721)
│   │ └ 8-Mary Thompson (1653-1691)
│   ┌ 6-Phebe Hawley (1726-   )
│   │ ┌ 8-Ichabod Stowe (1652-1695)
│   └ 7-Hope Stowe (1694-1763)
│   └ 8-Mary Atwater (1662-1746)
┌ 2- Charles Homer Fuller (1857-1927)
│   ┌ 8-Benjamin Hawley (1697-1765)
│   ┌ 7- William Hawley (1731-1791)
│   │ └ 8-Mary Nichols (1707-1767)
│   ┌ 6-Daniel Hawley (1776-   )
│   │ ┌ 8-John Glover (-   )
│   └ 7-Mary Glover (1752-   )

Figure 3a. Example of a Computer-Generated
Eight-Generation Ancestry Chart

Ancestry Chart of George Henry Fuller

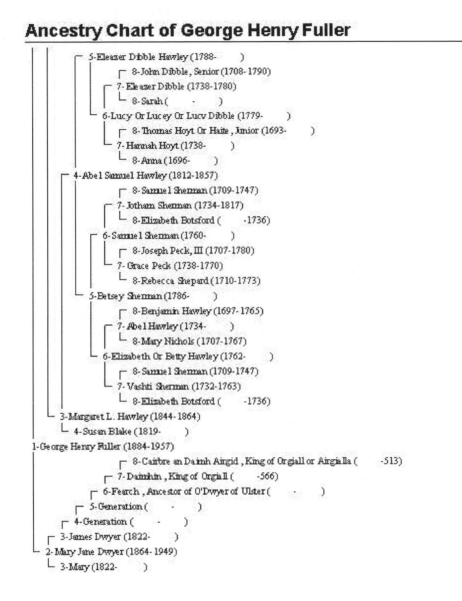

```
           ┌ 5-Eleazer Dibble Hawley (1788-        )
           │        ┌ 8-John Dibble, Senior (1708-1790)
           │  ┌ 7-Eleazer Dibble (1738-1780)
           │  │     └ 8-Sarah (        -        )
           │  └ 6-Lucy Or Lucey Or Lucy Dibble (1779-        )
           │        ┌ 8-Thomas Hoyt Or Haite, Junior (1693-        )
           │  ┌ 7-Hannah Hoyt (1738-        )
           │  │     └ 8-Anna (1696-        )
        ┌ 4-Abel Samuel Hawley (1812-1857)
        │  │        ┌ 8-Samuel Sherman (1709-1747)
        │  │  ┌ 7-Jotham Sherman (1734-1817)
        │  │  │     └ 8-Elizabeth Botsford (        -1736)
        │  └ 6-Samuel Sherman (1760-        )
        │     │        ┌ 8-Joseph Peck, III (1707-1780)
        │     └ 7-Grace Peck (1738-1770)
        │              └ 8-Rebecca Shepard (1710-1773)
        └ 5-Betsey Sherman (1786-        )
           │        ┌ 8-Benjamin Hawley (1697-1765)
           │  ┌ 7-Abel Hawley (1734-        )
           │  │     └ 8-Mary Nichols (1707-1767)
           └ 6-Elizabeth Or Betty Hawley (1762-        )
                    ┌ 8-Samuel Sherman (1709-1747)
              ┌ 7-Vashti Sherman (1732-1763)
                    └ 8-Elizabeth Botsford (        -1736)
     └ 3-Margaret L. Hawley (1844-1864)
        └ 4-Susan Blake (1819-        )
1-George Henry Fuller (1884-1957)
                    ┌ 8-Cairbre an Daimh Airgid, King of Orgiall or Airgialla (        -513)
              ┌ 7-Daimhin, King of Orgiall (        -566)
        ┌ 6-Fearch, Ancestor of O'Dwyer of Ulster (        -        )
     ┌ 5-Generation (        -        )
   ┌ 4-Generation (        -        )
 ┌ 3-James Dwyer (1822-        )
 └ 2-Mary Jane Dwyer (1864-1949)
    └ 3-Mary (1822-        )
```

Figure 3b. Example of a Computer-Generated Eight-Generation Ancestry Chart

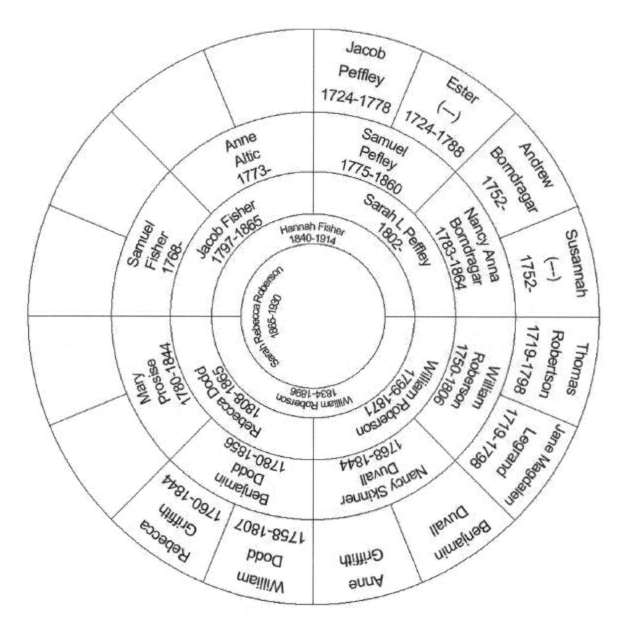

Figure 4. Example of a Computer-Generated Double Fan Chart

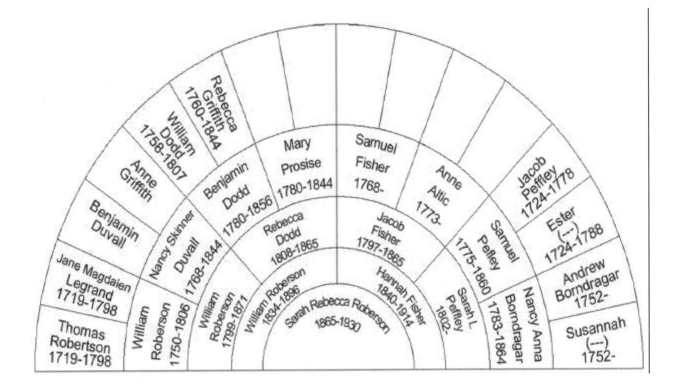

**Figure 5. Example of a Computer-Generated
Single Fan Chart**

Photographic Pedigree Chart

The fourth kind of preprinted blank pedigree chart is a photographic four-generation pedigree chart. There are preprinted boxes for small photographs of each individual on the pedigree chart.

The problem with this style of preprinted paper pedigree chart is that it is unlikely you will ever have photographs small enough to fit in the boxes without having special prints made. The adhesive substance you use to attach them does not last through the years, so pictures tend to fall off and the paper gets damaged. If you want to create a photographic style pedigree chart, it is best to use a software-generated version that includes the pictures in the correct size right on the printout.

Software-generated charts are created using your family history software and are automatically filled in as you enter data into family group sheets. The software eliminates the need to make double entries, which preprinted pedigree charts require. This eliminates errors in transcription. In the event you want to print a chart, you can decide if you want to include three to six generations, and—with some programs—even more. The more generations you add, the less information will appear for each generation. Most family history software programs now allow you to scan in photographs and include them automatically on your printed charts.

Pedigree Chart

No. 1 on this chart is the same as no. 1 on chart no. 1

8 Asa Clark Brown
b. 11 October 1792
p. Woodstock, Windham, Connecticut
m. 8 March 1832
p. Tionesta, Venango, Pennsylvania
d. 8 March 1866
p. Minneapolis, Hennepin, Minnesota

4 David Clark Brown
b. 24 November 1846
p. Deerfield, Warren, Pennsylvania
m. 1 January 1868
p. Brockway, Stearns, Minnesota
d. 9 February 1927
p. Everett, Snohomish, Washington

9 Eleanor Huppenan
b. 11 January 1803
p. Kingston, Frontenac, Ontario, Canada
d. 3 June 1874
p. Saint Cloud, Stearns, Minnesota

2 James David Brown
b. 8 May 1875
p. Saint Cloud, Stearns, Minnesota
m. 14 December 1899
p. Oak Park, Benton, Minnesota
d. 17 January 1929
p. Sipoco, Luzon Island, Phillipine Islands

10 Jonathan Crosby
b. 1825
p. Chanhassen, Carver, Minnesota
m.
p.
d. 1902
p. Deerfield, Warren, Pennsylvania

5 Clara Etta Crosby
b. 13 March 1850
p. Swanville, Waldo, Maine
d. 4 September 1928
p. Everett, Snohomish, Washington

11 Sarah Smart
b. 1829
p. Chanhassen, Carver, Minnesota
d. 7 May 1900
p. Deerfield, Warren, Pennsylvania

1 Jonathan Martin Brown
b. 16 June 1899
p. Akeley, Hubbard, Minnesota
m.
p.
d. 14 September 1969
p. Pendleton, Umatilla, Oregon
sp. Willma Mary McCall

12 Frank Williams
b.
p.
m.
p.
d.
p.

6 Donald G. Williams
b. 1845
p. Deerfield, Warren, Pennsylvania
m.
p.
d. Abt 1920
p. Akeley, Hubbard, Minnesota

13 Dorcas Cole
b. 1825
p.
d.
p.

3 Margaret May Williams
b. 10 May 1876
p. Osseo, Hennepin, Minnesota
d. 2 March 1907
p. Akeley, Hubbard, Minnesota

14 Lars Johansen
b. 1820
p.
m.
p.
d.
p.

7 Henrietta Johansen
b. 30 June 1849
p. Saint Cloud, Stearns, Minnesota
d.
p. Saint Cloud, Stearns, Minnesota

15 Anne
b.
p.
d.
p.

Figure 6. Example of a Computer-Generated Four-Generation Picture Pedigree Chart

Descendant Chart

Family history software can also create descendant charts showing all or a selected number of generations of descendants. The chart below illustrates a computer-generated chart that includes nine generations of descendants beginning with Sitre of Egypt.

Descendants of Sitre Of Egypt

Page 1

1- Sitre Of Egypt b: , Thebes, Uast, Waset, Egypt

+Ramses I Of Egypt, Pharaoh Of Egypt 19 Th Dynasty b: Abt 1345 B.C., Avaris, Nile Delta ,Egypt, d: Abt 1294 B.C., Thebes, Uast, Waset, Egypt

  2- Seti I Or Sety I Or MenMaat Re'sety Mer.En.Ptah Of Egypt, Pharaoh Of Egypt 19 Th Dynasty b: Abt 1323, Avaris, Nile Delta, Egypt, d: Abt 1279, Thebes, Uast, Waset, Egypt

  +Tuya , Queen Of Egypt b: , Thebes, Uast, Waset, Egypt

    3- Ramses II Or User.Maat.Re'setep.En.Re'ra.Messe Or Usermaatresetepenre Of Egypt, Pharaoh Of Egypt 19 Th Dynasty b: Abt 1302 B.C., Thebes, Uast, Waset, Egypt, d: Abt 1213 B.C., Thebes, Uast, Waset, Egypt

    +Nefertari Mery-En-Mut Of Egypt d: Abt 1254 B.C., Of Egypt

      4- Amen Hirkhopshef Or Amonherkhepeshef Or Amonhirwonmef Or Seth-Her-Khepeshef Of Egypt, Prince Of Egypt b: Abt 1275 B.C., , , Egypt

      4- Meryet-Amm

      4- Pa-Re-Her-Wenemef Of Egypt, Prince Of Egypt

      4- Mertatum Of Egypt

      4- Mery-Re Of Egypt b: Bef 1212 B.C., , , Egypt

      4- Mery-Atum

    +Isitnofret Of Egypt b: , Thebes, Uast, Waset, Egypt

      4- High Priest Of Ptah At Memphis, Kha'emweset Or Khaemwise Or Khaemwaset Of Egypt, Prince Of Egypt b: Abt 1272, Thebes, Uast, Waset, Egypt

      +Unknown

        5- Isitnofret Or Isinefre Of Egypt b: , Thebes, Uast, Waset, Egypt

      4- Merenptah Of Egypt, Pharaoh Of Egypt 19 Th Dynasty b: Abt 1273 B.C., Thebes, Uast, Waset, Egypt, d: 1202 B.C., (Kv 8, Deir-El-Bahri, Valley Of The Kings, Luxor, Egypt)

      +Isitnofret Or Isinefre Of Egypt b: , Thebes, Uast, Waset, Egypt

        5- Tiye-Mereniset Of Egypt b: , Thebes, Uast, Waset, Egypt

        5- 19th Dynasty, Seti II Or Sety-Merenptah Of Egypt, Pharaoh Of Egypt d: 1193 B.C., Tomb #55, Valley Of The Kings, Luxor, Egypt

      +Takah

        5- Amenmeses Of Egypt, Pharaoh of Egypt d: 1199 B.C., , , , Egypt

      4- Bant-Anta Or Bint-Anath

      +Ramses II Or User.Maat.Re'setep.En.Re'ra Messe Or Usermaatresetepenre Of Egypt, Pharaoh Of Egypt 19 Th Dynasty b: Abt 1302 B.C., Thebes, Uast, Waset, Egypt, d: Abt 1213 B.C., Thebes, Uast, Waset, Egypt

      4- Ramsses , Junior

    +Bant-Anta Or Bint-Anath

    +Nebt-Tawy

    +Herout-Mi-Re

    +Maathorneferure Or Maetnefrure Of Khatti, Princess Of Khatti Or Hittites b: , Hattusas ,Now, Bogazköy, Turkey

      4- Nakhte-Seti Or Setakht Or Siptah Of Egypt, Pharaoh Of Egypt 19 Th Dynasty b: Abt 1240 B.C., Thebes, Uast, Waset, Egypt, d: Abt 1184 B.C., Thebes, Uast, Waset, Egypt

      +Tiye-Mereniset Of Egypt b: , Thebes, Uast, Waset, Egypt

        5- Ramses III Usimaere Of Egypt Of Egypt, Paharaoh Of Egypt 20 Th Dynasty b: Abt 1217 B.C., d: Abt 1151 B.C., Medinet Habu, Valley Of The Kings, Luxor, Egypt

    +Bentresh Or Ma'at Hornefrure , Princess Of Bekhtan

    +Ueret-Ma-A-Neferu-Ra b: , Thebes, Uast, Waset, Egypt

Figure 7. Example of a Descendancy Chart

210

Entering Information on a Blank Pedigree Chart

The first individual on the first pedigree chart is you. If you are filling out a paper version, be sure to use black ink. Follow your own information with your parents' information in the spaces provided for the next generation. The spaces provided for the generation after that are for information about their parents. Males are always entered first, followed by their spouse for each generation. The marriage date and place will be entered under the male for each couple. You will be in position 1 on chart 1, followed by your parents (numbered 2 and 3 on chart number 1), and so on until you have 15 individuals entered on the first chart (assuming you are doing a 15-person chart).

Each paper chart has blank lines after each individual in the fourth generation. These will be filled in, on the first chart page, with numbers 2 through 9 as you continue each line onto another pedigree chart page. These numbers are called extension numbers. They tell you what chart number to look on for the next generation.

Each paper chart also has a way of linking back to the previous chart. These are called cross-reference numbers. They tell you where to find the first individual appearing on this chart on a previous chart. When you have acquired thousands of names, this information becomes quite important in order to navigate to a previous generation.

Software-generated pedigree charts and FGRs work the same way but use a different numbering system. The first individual you enter into your database is automatically given the record identification number, or RIN, of 1. Each person you enter into the database is given a successive and unique RIN. Each married couple is given their own unique marriage record identification number or MRIN (for more information, see Unique Numbering Systems on page 214). Any individual in the database can be set as the first individual to appear on a pedigree chart. This individual is called the root person. Once this individual is selected, the pedigree chart will identify all ancestors and descendents and fill out the pedigree chart automatically for you. By using the RIN and MRIN numbers, your software links the father, mother, children, and grandparents together. These numbers will be included in every GEDCOM file you create from your database.

Pedigree Chart for

No. 1 on this chart is the same as no. _____ on chart no. _____   Chart no. _____

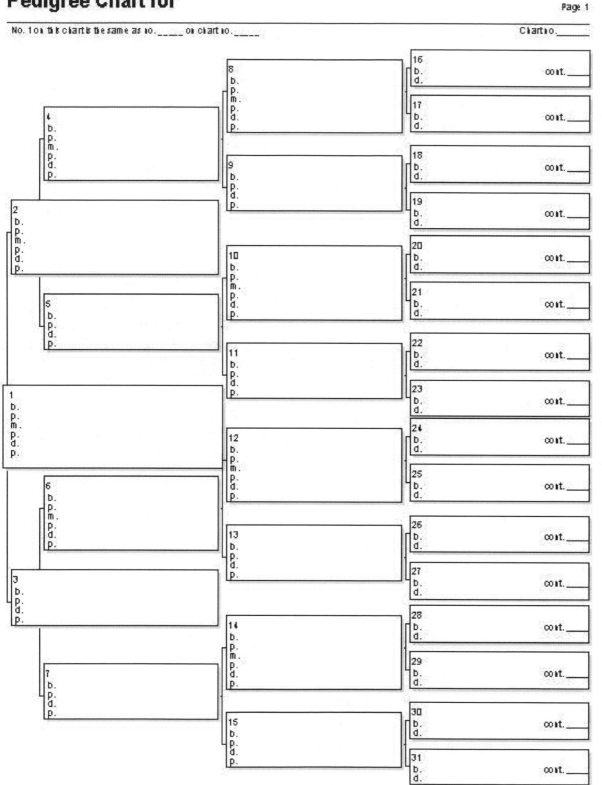

Figure 8. Example of a Blank Pedigree Chart

Organizing Computerized FGRs and Pedigree Charts

Since your computer program will automatically organize your data for you, there are only a few items to consider as you organize your information. The two major areas to consider are hard disk space or storage space for your information and the time it will take to access that information in an effective manner.

Disk Space

First, most family history software limits the number of individuals you can enter into your software to a specific number of individuals or by the size of your hard disk storage space. Also, the more scanned documents and pictures or other information you enter in the notes and events fields of your software per individual, the less storage space you will have for adding more individuals. Determine the amount of storage capacity you will need for your software and your database, including the amount of storage space you will need for scanned documents and pictures. The simplest solution to limited storage space is to get a larger hard drive. The second is to store scanned items on multiple diskettes, tapes, or recordable optical media such as the various kinds of recordable digital video discs (DVD) or compact discs (CD). Recordable CDs are like CD-ROMs (read-only memory) except that you can record on them and, depending on the format, effectively erase or rewrite the data, similar to what you can do with a diskette (only with far greater capacity). Recordable disc drives and CDs for your computer vary in their speed, compatibility, longevity, and capacity, so it is best to research these technologies before purchasing a system.

Accessing and Searching Your Database

You will want to manage the amount of time you spend searching in your database for an ancestor. Initially, when you have only a few names or even a few hundred names, this is not a problem. But as your database size grows, so do your search, sort, editing, and retrieval times. In some programs, as your database exceeds 50,000 names it may seem like your computer is crawling, and when you get to 250,000 names you may wonder why you ever abandoned your paper copies. Adding random access memory (RAM) to your computer is the best solution and should help these problems in most cases. There is another, slightly more difficult to manage, solution if adding more RAM is not an option for you: multiple databases.

Initially set up two databases, one for your father's information and one for your mother's. This will divide your current database in half and may work better for your software's or computer's limitations. As your database grows, you can further divide your databases making one for each grandparent. If you keep your information on your surname line in your primary database, you will always know how each of the four smaller databases fit together. These lines can then be easily recombined for publication of reports and books. This can be a cumbersome solution, but it does make it possible to use older computers that have limited amounts of RAM, allowing them to perform better when using all the major family history software packages.

Unique Numbering Systems

Before the invention of family history software, numerous numbering conventions were created to keep track of individuals in family lines and the publication of books. Family history software automatically assigns a unique number to each individual in your database referred to as a Record Identification Number, or RIN for short. Each married couple is assigned a Marriage Record Identification Number or MRIN. These numbers allow your software to keep track of relationships so you can view and print family group records, pedigree charts and books without confusion.

The following is a short list of the most popular numbering systems used by hobbyists and professionals, ranging from very simple to quite complex. At times, these styles have been combined to create even more complex systems. Now they are predominantly used only in family history book publishing. Arguments have raged through the years as to which is the best method to use, and different publishing houses seem to have settled on formats they each prefer. The use of unique numbering systems is optional. Use is based on personal preferences.

Table 21. Frequently Used Numbering Systems

Ahnentafel or Soza-Stradonitz	Modified Henry
D'Aboville	*Modified Register or Report
De Villiers	*NGSQ
Henry	*Register (NEHGS)
Modified De Villiers Pama	

* Indicates prefered numbering systems for publication

If you choose to use one of the above numbering systems in addition to your computer-generated RINs and MRINs, the additional numbers are entered in the user identification field. Most family history software now allows you to sort and publish based on these numbers.

Example of computer-generated RINs and User Identification Numbers

Your computer software automatically assigns a RIN when an individual record is created.

Individual's Information [11452]

Given Sylvester
Last Van Noordwijck

Title Pre.		Title Suf.	
Born	13 Jul 1888	in	Roche			113
Chr.	27 Aug 1888	in	Saint Ambrose Church, Rochester, Monroe Co		
Died	11 Apr 1944	in	Webster, Monroe, New York, USA		55
Bur.	13 Apr 1944	in	Webster, Monroe, New York, USA		55

User ID# 1809   AFN ZXXC-89   Living? Yes No

Save
Cancel

Optional numbering systems such as any of the following are entered in the User ID field: Ahnentafel or Soza-Stradonitz, D'Aboville, De Villiers, Henry, Modified De Villiers Pama, Modified Henry, Modified Register or Report, Register (NEHGS), or NGSQ Systems.

Example of computer-generated FGR showing use of RINs and MRINs

Family Group Record -45053

Husband	William II De Montague, King of Isle of Man-[118421]		
AKA	William De Montacute 3rd Baron Montacute., William Montacute 3rd Baron of Montacute, William De Salsbury 1S~		
Born	1302-1303	Cassington, Oxfordshire, England	
Christened			
Died	30 Jan 1343-1344	Windsor Castle, Windsor, Berkshire, England	
Buried			
Father	William I De Montague, Baron Montague, 2nd Lord Montacute-[125330] (1275-1319)		
Mother	Elizabeth De Montfort-[125317] (1271-1345)		
Married	1327	Cassington, Oxfordshire, England	
Wife	**Katherine De Grandeson-[125487]**		
AKA	Katherine Grandison		
Born	Abt 1304	Ashford, Hertfordshire, England	
Christened			
Died	23 Nov 1349	Bisham, Berkshire, England	
Buried			
Father	William De Grandeson, Lord Grandeson-[125488] (1255-1335)		
Mother	Sybil De Tregoze-[125489] (1270-1334)		
Father	William , Lord Grandison-[170804] (Abt 1276-		
Mother	Sibella De Tergoz-[171499] (Abt 1279-)		
Children			
1 F	Elizabeth De Montague-[125500]		
Born	Abt 1325	Of, Donyatt, Somersetshire, England	
Christened			
Died	31 May 1359	Ashley, Hampshire, England	
Buried			
Spouse	Giles De Badlesmere-[119527] (1314-1338)	After Feb 1327-1328, Donyatt, Somersetshire, England	
Spouse	Le Despenser-[118417] (Abt 1333-1374)	Bef 27 Apr 1341, Of, Donyatt, Somersetshire, England	
Spouse	Of Bryan, Lord Bryan-[144810] (Abt 1318-1390)	Bef 10 Jul 1350, Of, Donyatt, Somersetshire, England	
2 M	John De Montague, Baron Montague-[125450]		

Each individual is given a unique record identification number, or RIN.

Organizing Paper FGR Forms and Pedigree Charts

The simplest way to organize paper FGR forms is to place them in alphabetical order by surname and then by given name, followed by date of birth, oldest to youngest. Pedigree charts should be organized numerically. By using this method, you have two ways to access your data. First, if you identify your ancestor on a pedigree chart, you can then locate them in the paper FGR form as the spouse or as the child. Second, you can directly access them alphabetically. This is especially helpful when you have found a piece of data on, say, a William Alexander but you happen to have fifteen people with the same name. If your records are organized alphabetically, these people will all be listed together so you can readily find the correct one, instead of having to identify each line they belong to before you can find the right ancestor to enter the new data.

III. Research Logs

After you enter all the information that you can acquire from living relatives, you will begin the process of looking for other records about your ancestors. Research logs are used to keep track of the resources that you have searched as well as the results of your activities.

A research log is made for each surname, ancestor, and location researched. Some professional researchers keep research logs for each kind of resource, allowing fast access to source materials for the next client.

Perform the following steps:

1. Enter the family surname, the full name of the individual, or the full geographic description of the location being researched.

2. Enter the goal of your research.

3. Enter the date you conducted your research. This will help you identify not only when you did the research, but also which research trip you were on when you accessed the information.

4. Enter the name of the repository where you found your source. Include the name, address, telephone number, hours of operation, web address, and any other information that will help you if you have to find and access this source again. Include Dewey decimal call numbers, information on special collections of historical materials, locations (department names, floor numbers, etc.) within buildings, microfilm and microfiche reel and frame numbers, and the full citation of the resource (including the name of the author, compiler, or editor; the title; the publisher; the date of publication; the city in which the piece was published; and the page numbers searched).

5. Enter detailed results of your research. Include notes, even if a particular source was totally fruitless. This will prevent you from looking at the same source at a later date. By entering very detailed information you will be better able to conduct further research, order additional resources such as microfilm and microfiche, and obtain books from repositories such as Family History Resource centers and the New England Historical Society's book-lending library.

Example of how to complete a research log

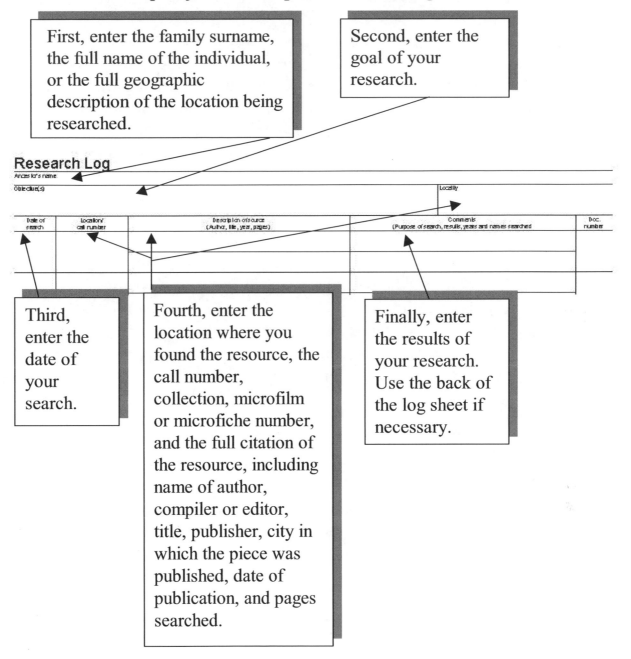

First, enter the family surname, the full name of the individual, or the full geographic description of the location being researched.

Second, enter the goal of your research.

Third, enter the date of your search.

Fourth, enter the location where you found the resource, the call number, collection, microfilm or microfiche number, and the full citation of the resource, including name of author, compiler or editor, title, publisher, city in which the piece was published, date of publication, and pages searched.

Finally, enter the results of your research. Use the back of the log sheet if necessary.

IV. Correspondence Logs

While compiling genealogical information about your ancestor, it may become necessary to write to others for additional information. A correspondence log is essential to help you keep track of all letters and e-mail inquiries regarding your ancestor. It is preferable for all correspondence to be typed or computer-generated. When this is not possible, inquiries regarding your ancestor should be written in black ink on white, acid-free paper if hand written. It is customary to include a self-addressed stamped envelope (SASE) with your return address.

Although there is not one standardized form to use, the following items are typically included in a correspondence log:

- Name of ancestor or family being researched.
- A copy of your correspondence.
- The date your correspondence was sent.
- The name and address or e-mail address of the addressee.
- The purpose of your correspondence.
- The date of reply.
- The results of your inquiry.
- Fees paid or owed, if applicable.

Most family history software now includes correspondence logs as a program feature. Also typically included are to-do lists and further research lists in conjunction with the correspondence logs to help you keep track of your progress and pending tasks.

Appendix A. Roman Numerals

Roman Numeral	Arabic Equivalent	Roman Numeral	Arabic Equivalent
I	1	XC or LXXXX	90
II	2	C	100
III	3	CC	200
IV or IIII	4	CCC	300
V	5	CD or CCCC	400
VI	6	D	500
VII	7	DC	600
VIII	8	DCC	700
IX or VIIII	9	DCCC	800
X	10	CM or DCCCC	900
XX	20	M	1000
XXX	30	MD	1500
XL or XXXX	40	MDC	1600
L	50	MDCC	1700
LX	60	MDCCC	1800
LXX	70	MCM	1900
XXC or LXXX	80	MM	2000

Appendix B. LDS Temple Codes by City

Temple Code	Temple Code Old	City, Province	State or Country
ABA		Aba	Nigeria
ACCRA		Accra	Ghana
ADELA		Adelaide	Australia
ALBER	AL	Cardston, Alberta	Canada
ALBUQ		Albuquerque	New Mexico
ANCHO		Anchorage	Alaska
APIA	AP	Apia	Western Samoa
ASUNC		Asunción	Paraguay
ARIZO	AZ	Mesa	Arizona
ATLAN	AT	Atlanta	Georgia
BAIRE	BA	Buenos Aires	Argentina
BILLI		Billings	Montana
BIRMI		Birmingham	Alabama
BISMA		Bismarck	North Dakota
BOGOT	BG	Bogota	Colombia
BOSIE	BO	Boise	Idaho
BOSTO		Boston	Massachusetts
BOUNT	N/A	Bountiful	Utah
BRISB		Brisbane	Australia
BROUG		Baton Rouge	Louisiana
CAMPI		Campinas	Brazil
CARAC		Caracas D.F.	Venezuela
CHICA	CH	Chicago	Illinois
CIUJU		Ciudad Juárez	Mexico
COCHA		Cochabamba	Bolivia
COLJU		Colonia Juárez Chihuahua	Mexico
COLSC		Columbia	South Carolina
CRIVE		Columbia River	Washington
COLUM		Columbus	Ohio
COPEN		Copenhagen	Denmark
DALLA	DA	Dallas	Texas
DENVE	DV	Denver	Colorado
DETRO		Detroit	Michigan

EDMON		Edmonton, Alberta	Canada
EHOUS	EH	Endowment House	
FRANK	FR	Frankfurt	Germany
FREIB	FD	Freiberg	Germany
FRESN		Fresno	California
FUKUO		Fukuoka	Japan
GUADA		Guadalajara	Mexico
GUATE	GU	Guatemala	Guatemala
GUAYA	GY	Guayaquil	Ecuador
HAGUE		The Hague	Netherlands
HALIF		Halifax, Nova Scotia	Canada
HELSI		Helsinki	Finland
HAWAI		Laie	Hawaii
HERMO		Hermosillo Sonora	Mexico
HKONG		Hong Kong	China
HOUST		Houston	Texas
IFALL	IF	Idaho Falls	Idaho
JOHAN	JO	Johannesburg	South Africa
JRIVE	JR	Jordan River	Utah
KIEV		Kiev	Ukraine
N/A		Kirtland[17]	Ohio
KONA		Kona	Hawaii
LANGE	LA	Los Angeles	California
LIMA	LI	Lima	Peru
LOGAN	LG	Logan	Utah
LONDO	LD	London	England
LOUIS		Louisville	Kentucky
LVEGA	LV	Las Vegas	Nevada
LUBBO		Lubbock	Texas
MADRI		Madrid	Spain
MANIL	MA	Manila	Philippines
MANTI	MT	Manti	Utah
MEDFO		Medford	Oregon
MELBO		Melbourne	Australia
MEMPH		Memphis	Tennessee
MERID		Mérdia	Yucatán
MEXIC	MX	Mexico City D.F.	Mexico

---

[17] The Church of Jesus Christ of Latter-day Saints no longer owns the Kirtland Temple.

MNTVD		Montevideo	Uruguay
MONTE		Monterrey	Mexico
MONTI		Monticello	Utah
MONTR		Montreal, Quebec	Canada
MTIMP		Mount Timpanogos	Utah
NASHV		Nashville	Tennessee
NAUV2		Nauvoo (new)	Illinois
NAUVO	NV	Nauvoo (original)	Illinois
NBEAC		Newport Beach	California
NUKUA	TG	Nuku'alofa	Tonga
NYORK		Harrison	New York
NZEAL		Hamilton	New Zealand
OAKLA	OK	Oakland	California
OAXAC		Oaxaca	Mexico
OGDEN	OG	Ogden	Utah
OKLAH		Oklahoma City	Oklahoma
ORLAN		Orlando	Florida
OTHER			
PALEG		Porto Alegre	Brazil
PALMY		Palmyra	New York
PAPEE	TA	Papeete	Tahiti
PERTH		Perth	Australia
POFFI	PO	President's Office	
PORTL	PT	Portland	Oregon
PREST		Preston	England
PROVO	PV	Provo	Utah
RALEI		Raleigh	North Carolina
RECIF		Recife	Brazil
REDLA		Redlands	California
REGIN		Regina, Saskatchewan	Canada
RENO		Reno	Nevada
SACRA		Sacramento	California
ANTON		San Antonio	Texas
SANTI	SN	Santiago	Chile
SDIEG	SA	San Diego	California
SDOMI		Santo Domingo	Dominican Republic
SEATT	SE	Seattle	Washington
SEOUL	SO	Seoul	South Korea
SGEOR	SG	Saint George	Utah

SJOSE		San Jose	Costa Rica
SLAKE	SL	Salt Lake City	Utah
SLOUI		Saint Louis	Missouri
SPAUL	SP	São Paulo	Brazil
SPMIN		Saint Paul	Minnesota
SNOWF		Snowflake	Arizona
SPOKA		Spokane	Washington
STOCK	ST	Stockholm	Sweden
SUVA		Suva	Fiji
SWISS	SW	Bern	Switzerland
SYDNE	SD	Sydney	Australia
TAIPE	TP	Taipei	Taiwan
TAMPI		Tampico	Mexico
TGUTI		Tuxtia Gutierrez	Mexico
TOKYO	TK	Tokyo	Japan
TORON	TR	Toronto, Ontario	Canada
VERAC		Veracruz	Mexico
VERNA		Vernal	Utah
VILLA		Vilahermosa Tabasco	Mexico
WASHI	WA	Washington	D.C.
WINTE		Winter Quarters (new)	Nebraska
WQUAR	WQ	Winter Quarters (original)	Nebraska

Appendix C. World's Major Religions and Subdivisions

Agnosticism	
Atheism	
Baha'i	
Buddhism	
	Jodo Shinshu Japanese
	Mahayana Buddhist
	Nichiren Shoshu of America
	Nyingmapa Tibetan
	Theravada
	Vajrayana
	Zen
Christian	
	Advent Christian
	Anabaptist
	Apostolic
	Assembly of God
	Baptist
	Baptist ABA
	Baptist American
	Baptist Bible Fellowship
	Baptist Conservative
	Baptist Free Will
	Baptist General Conference
	Baptist Independent
	Baptist Missionary
	Baptist Reformed
	Baptist Seventh Day
	Baptist Southern
	Bible Christians (refer to Methodists, below)
	Byzantine Catholic
	Roman Catholic
	Calvinist
	Campbellite
	Charismatic

	Church of Christ
	Christian Reformed
	Christian Scientist
	Church of England—Anglican
	Church of God
	Church of Jesus Christ of Latter-day Saints
	Congregation of the Unity of Brethren
	Congregationalist
	Cumberland Presbyterian Church
	Deist
	Disciples of Christ
	Dutch Reformed
	Eastern Orthodox
	Emmanuelist
	Episcopal
	Episcopal Missionary
	Episcopal Reformed
	Evangelical
	Evangelical Covenant
	Evangelical Free
	Evangelical Methodist
	Fellowship of Christian Assemblies
	Free Methodist
	Friends, Society of—Quaker
	Full Gospel
	Fundamentalist
	German Reformed
	Grace Brethren
	Hispanic—Hosanna Asamblea De Dios
	Holiness
	Independent
	Independent Bible
	Inghamite
	Interdenominational
	Jehovah's Witness
	Jewish Christian
	Lutheran

	Lutheran Missouri Synod
	Lutheran Wisconsin Evangelical Synod
	Mennonite
	Mennonite Brethren
	Methodist African Episcopal
	Methodist Church
	Methodist Episcopal
	Methodist Free
	Methodist Independent (refer also to United Churches of Christ)
	Methodist Primitive (refer after 1932 to Methodist Church)
	Methodist United (refer after 1932 to Methodist Church)
	Millennialism
	Millerites
	Moravians (refer also to Congregation of the Unity of Brethren)
	Nazarene
	New Church (refer to Swedenborgians)
	New Jerusalemites (refer to Swedenborgians)
	Nondenominational
	Open Bible Standard
	Pentecostal
	Pentecostal Church of God
	Pentecostal Holiness
	Pentecostal United
	Presbyterian
	Presbyterian Church in America
	Presbyterian Evangelical
	Presbyterian Orthodox
	Protestant
	Protestant Episcopal Church
	Puritanism
	Reorganized Church of Jesus Christ of Latter-Day Saints
	Revivalist
	Russian Orthodox

	Salvation Army
	Schwenkfelders
	Seventh-day Adventist
	Swedenborgians
	United Society of Believers in Christ's Second Coming—Shaker
	Unitarian
	United Brethren—Moravian
	United Church of Christ
	Unity
	Universalism
Confucianism	
Jainism	
Jedi	
Hinduism	
Islam	
	Shi'ite
	Sufi
	Sunni
Judaism	
	Ashkenazim
	Sephardim
	Hasidim
	Mitnagdim
	Modern Orthodox
	Conservative
	Reformed
	Assimilated
	Zionist
Krishna Consciousness	
Metaphysical	
Mysticism	
Native American Church	
Natural Religionist	Use Natural Religionist for those who worship nature.

Neo-paganism	Use Neo-paganism to include revivalists of pre-Christian religions of Greece and Rome, Witches, Druids, Goddess Worshippers, and other pagan forms of worship.
New Age	
New Thought	
Personality Cultist	
Religious Science	
Science of Mind	
Scientology	
Self Realization	
Shinto	
	Shinto Fuso-kyo
	Shinto Izumo Taisha-kyo
	Shinto Konko-kyo
	Shinto Kurozumi-kyo
	Shinto Jikkyo-kyo
	Shinto Misogi-kyo
	Shinto Ontake-kyo
	Shinto Shinri-kyo
	Shinto Shinshu-kyo
	Shinto Shusei-ha
	Shinto Taisei-kyo
	Shinto Tenri-kyo
Sikhism	
Spiritualism	
Taoism	
Voodooism	
	Voodoo
Zoroastrianism	
	Zurvanism

Appendix D. Other Languages in Your Software

To be able to enter family names or other text in different written languages into your family history database, the software you use must provide support for the alphabet or characters of that language. This section provides a brief overview of some of the software features and settings you may need, depending on your software and the language you want to enter and display.[18]

Note that as of this printing, most family history software programs available do not support non-Latin alphabets. Until the necessary support becomes available in these programs, you will need to record information in such languages on paper.

Refer to your family history software and operating system software documentation or online help as needed for details on installing any software or features, or changing language settings that may be needed to support other languages. The information below is a general overview of what may be involved depending on the language, your family history software, and the operating system in your computer.

Latin Alphabet

Your software may already support the other languages you need without making any changes. Besides English, characters used in European and other languages can often be inserted into records directly using your family history software, or using a simple utility program such as Character Map (included with the Windows operating system, in the Accessories folder).

For extensive data entry involving other languages using the Latin alphabet, you may want to install the correct keyboard layout file for the language. The correct keyboard layout enables you to use keys on your standard keyboard to enter the characters for a given language that are not normally accessible directly from your keyboard. The keyboard layout file comes with or is available for your particular operating system and language. For example, in versions of the Windows operating system, the keyboard layout can be selected using the Keyboard applet. Find the Keyboard icon in the Control Panel by selecting Start (Windows 95 or greater), then double-clicking Control Panel. When the Control Panel folder opens, double-

---

[18] Note that this section refers to support for various characters and script as used in written languages that you may wish to enter into your database, see displayed on your screen, share online, or print on a printer. It does not pertain to the language(s) in which your software *user interface* is presented, which is typically English but can be different from the data you input or display about your ancestors.

click the Keyboard icon. Then, select the Input Locales tab. From there, you can select the available keyboard layouts installed on your computer.

Unicode Support

The ability to store and display information using the correct characters or script for any language supported by your computer's operating system—and virtually every known written language on this planet—is called support for the Unicode standard. Unicode is an international standard that is or will be supported by every major operating system and modern multilanguage software program or database. If you or others with whom you share files will be using non-Latin alphabets at some point in your family history research, you will want Unicode support in both your operating system software (e.g., recent versions of Microsoft Windows) and your family history software.

Unicode support is the foundational standard needed to work compatibly with all written languages on your computer; however, you can upgrade your software to support this feature in the future when you need it and when it is available without having to manually convert any of your computerized data. While all software and online databases do not support Unicode today, it will be supported in GEDCOM files and family history software and online databases in the future. Even if you do not need it today, as your family history extends back in time you may come across the need for Unicode support in your software at some point in your research, so keep this in mind when upgrading your family history software.

Language Support Features

Depending on the language and version of your computer's operating system software, you may need to install the included operating system features called multi-language support or language support for a given language. For example, to enter characters from the Baltic, Central European, Cyrillic, Greek, or Turkish alphabets, you will need to install the operating system language support for the desired language (unless you are already using a version of the operating system in that language). Likewise, for "right to left" languages such as Arabic, Hebrew, Farsi, and Urdu, you will need to install the operating system's language support feature for that language (again, unless you are using a version of the operating system in that language). In addition to installing the needed language support in your operating system, you will want to make sure your family history software or word processor supports or plans to support the languages you will be using.

232

Fonts

You will need fonts installed that include the characters of the language or writing system for which you wish to enter or display information in your software. Fonts already on your computer support the Latin character sets used by most western languages. However, other languages may require installing new fonts if you have not already installed software that supports those languages. For example, most English-language fonts do not include Chinese characters, so if you will be entering Chinese names or notes, you will need (in addition to Unicode support) a font that includes these characters. Suitable fonts are probably included and installed with your family history software if it supports a given language requiring them. Installation of such fonts may be an optional choice during setup, so refer to your software documentation as needed. Other programs that support multiple languages, such as more recent versions of Microsoft Office, may also have installed the necessary fonts for a given writing system when you installed those programs on your computer. Fonts installed with one program will typically work with other programs that use the same character sets, regardless of the order in which the software was installed.

Asian Languages

For Asian languages (e.g., Simplified Chinese, Traditional Chinese, Japanese, and Korean), you may need to install additional software to facilitate the entering of ideographic characters of that language using a standard keyboard. This software is commonly called an Input Method Editor (IME) for a given language. An IME is a program that converts your keystrokes into the characters of the desired ideographic language. Again, this software may be included with your family history software, operating system, or other software you already use. Refer to your software documentation or online help for details.

Appendix E. Gazetteers and Maps

A gazetteer is an alphabetical dictionary of place names that contains descriptive geographical and other information about the places included. Gazetteers can help you identify the parent county or original territory of a locale, which will help you locate records. They also provide the correct spelling of a place name, and may help you determine any historical changes in boundaries, identify other places with the same place name, determine distances from nearby places, identify and locate civil and ecclesiastical jurisdictions, and likewise help identify and locate church meeting houses and the denominations of those churches. Gazetteers typically list the population of a locale and may include maps or other illustrations.

Maps and collections of maps (atlases) are illustrations of geographically, politically, or otherwise delineated areas that may help indicate the location of place names in relationship to other place names, mileage calculations, and points of interest in family history research. Maps may denote village, city, town, county, and state or province boundaries. They also may depict major traveling routes, public facilities (including government buildings), churches, and cemeteries, as well as geographical features such as lakes, rivers, and historical landmarks.

Both gazetteers and maps can provide invaluable clues to aid you in ongoing research. When using information from either of these sources, a full citation is entered into the Source field.

The following gazetteers may prove helpful if you are researching in the British Isles. All of them may be found in the Family History Library, Salt Lake City, Utah. Some may be ordered from gazetteer suppliers:

Bartholomew, *Gazetteer of the British Isles,* 1972
Census of Ireland 1871 – Alphabetical Listing to the Towns and Townlands of Ireland, 1877
Groome, *Ordinance Gazetteer of Scotland,* 1884
Lewis, *Topographical Dictionary of England,* 1831
Lewis, *Topographical Dictionary of Ireland,* 1837
Lewis, *Topographical Dictionary of Wales,* 1840
Names of Streets and Places in the Administrative County of London, 1955
Phillimore Atlas and Index of Parish Registers England and Wales, 1984

Richards, *Welsh Administrative and Territorial Units,* 1969
Smith, *Genealogical Gazetteer of England,* 1968
Wilson, *Imperial Gazetteer of England and Wales,* 1870
Wilson, *Gazetteer of Scotland,* 1882

Gazetteers and maps may be purchased from:

Genealogy Unlimited, Inc. P.O. Box 537 Orem, Utah 84059-0537 (801) 226-8971 (800) 666-4363	Stevenson's Genealogical Center 230 West 1230 North Provo, Utah 84604 (801) 374-9600
Deseret Book Company 40 East South Temple Street Salt Lake City, Utah 84130 (801) 534-1515 (800) 453-4532	Everton Publishers Box 368 Logan, Utah 84323-0368 (800) 443-6325
Ancestry, Inc. P.O. Box 476 350 South 400 East, Suite 10 Salt Lake City, Utah 84110 (800) 262-3787	Genealogical Publishing Company, Inc. 1001 North Calvert Street Baltimore, Maryland 21202 (800) 296-6687
Jonathan Sheppard Books Box 2020 ESP Station Albany, New York 12230	The Gold Bug P.O. Box 588 Alamo, California 94507-0588 (510) 838-6277
The Rand McNally Map Company P.O. Box 7600 Chicago, Illinois 60680 (800) 333-0134	American Map Company 46-35 54th Road Maspeth, New York 11278 (714) 784-0055

Appendix F. Other Resources

Free Software

At the time of this printing, *Legacy Family Tree Software* may be downloaded free of charge from Millennia Corporation at http://legacyfamilytree.com/. This is a full-featured professional genealogy program that helps you track, organize, print, and share your family history. It includes sourcing, reports, merging, To Do list, slide shows, multimedia, Web pages, spell checking, import and export and much more.

Personal Ancestral File may be downloaded free of charge from The Church of Jesus Christ of Latter-day Saints at http://www.familysearch.org/Eng/default.asp. This is a basic family history program that now includes the ability to view screens and print reports in English, German, Japanese, Chinese, Korean, or Swedish.

Books

Clifford, Karen. *Becoming an Accredited Genealogist: 100 Tips to Ensure Your Success.* Salt Lake City: Ancestry, 1998.

Litchman, William M. *"Applying for Certification? It's Worth It!"* APGQ 11 (September 1996).

Mills, Elizabeth Shown, Paul F. Smart, Jimmy B. Parker, and Claire Mire Bettag. *Professional Genealogy: A Manual for Researchers, Writers, Editors, Lecturers, and Librarians.* Baltimore: Genealogical Publishing Co., 2001

Mills, Elizabeth Shown *Evidence: Citation and Analysis for the Family Historian.* Baltimore: Genealogical Publishing Co., 1997

Stevenson, Noel C., *Genealogical Evidence: A Guide to the Standard of Proof Relating to Pedigrees, Ancestry, Heirship and Family History.* Laguna Hills, CA: Aegean Park Press, 1989

Index

H

N

255